CAPTAIN BUCKO'S NAUTI-WORDS HANDBOOK

CAPTAIN BUCKO'S NAUTI-WORDS HANDBOOK

Fascinating Facts and Fables About the Origins of Hundreds of Nautical Terms and Everyday Expressions

Roger Paul Huff

iUniverse, Inc.
New York Lincoln Shanghai

Captain Bucko's Nauti-Words Handbook
Fascinating Facts and Fables About the Origins of Hundreds of Nautical
Terms and Everyday Expressions

iUniverse, Inc.

For information address:
iUniverse, Inc.
2021 Pine Lake Road, Suite 100
Lincoln, NE 68512
www.iuniverse.com

Front Cover Artwork by R.F. Zogbaum Courtesy of the Naval Historical Center

ISBN: 0-595-31529-1

Printed in the United States of America

"To Gus, The Golden Retriever"

ACKNOWLEDGEMENTS

Every reasonable effort has been made to determine that any non-original graphics are in the public domain, except if otherwise noted. Wherever applicable, permission for usage has been obtained and credit has been indicated in the accompanying text.

The author would like to acknowledge and thank the US Navy, Coast Guard, Naval Historical Center, his shipmates, friends, family, and others without whose support writing this would have been like using the weather head in a fresh breeze. May you always have fair winds and following seas!

FOREWORD

Etymology—The *New Webster Encyclopedic Dictionary of the English Language* seems to be under an impression that this odd word refers to something called "philology," but Captain Bucko knows that this is actually the nautical term for studying the incredible *Etym,* a once common sea creature that became extinct because its name sounded too much like "Eat him!" None of you bought this handbook because you wanted more philology in your life, but because you were curious about the nautical origins of everyday expressions and fascinating backgrounds of the strange nautical words.

✳
IT'S TIME TO MEET THE CAPTAIN!
✳

But Captain Bucko is not your typical academic Etymologist. With almost fifty years of nautical experiences including a career as a professional oceanographer, he has owned and operated a variety of watercraft upon rivers, lakes, bayous, and oceans around the globe. He has dived for sunken treasure ships, and has swum with alligators and sea snakes. He has done research on sharks, and worked on underwater habitat and deepwater salvage operations. He has even been stranded on a deserted island, and partied with natives wearing a loincloth. Over these years he has collected hundreds of nautical terms and expressions from many sources, ranging from naval personnel and merchant mariners to some characters that hang out in waterfront bars (and yacht clubs) from New England to Micronesia. And unlike most Etymologists, Captain Bucko actually has a sense of humor!

✻

THIS HAS SOMETHING FOR EVERYONE!

✻

Landlubbers will be utterly amazed to discover how many words and phrases they routinely use have nautical origins. Armed with *Captain Bucko's Nauti-Words Handbook*, novice boaters will no longer be embarrassed for not understanding the meanings of obscure nautical terms used by the blowhard at their marina with the $9.99 yachting cap, sweatshirt that reads "Captain," and large, obnoxious green parrot named Barnacle Bill that periodically shrieks, "Arrgh!"

Even "old salts" are likely to learn something new. And if you already know the backgrounds of all the words and phrases in this handbook, it is time to put an oar on your shoulder and start walking inland until you get to somewhere the locals ask, "Hey Buddy, what's that thing on your shoulder?"

✻

WHY THIS HANDBOOK IS DIFFERENT

✻

Others may focus on one facet (e.g., early sailing terms), but this handbook covers a broader range of words and phrases in a uniquely humorous style. Less entertaining publications may sometime claim to be complete, authoritative sources for nautical terms. Bilge water! Captain Bucko does not claim to be an ultimate authority on anything, and he fully expects to live up to this claim.

✻

THE TIME HAS COME TO BOARD

✻

Captain Bucko's Nauti-Words Handbook includes approximately 800 terms and expressions, plus some *Handy Hints* and *Trivial Tidbits*. Do not attempt to read all of it in one sitting, or your brain may overheat. However, since the contents are arranged in alphabetical order, you might wish to review the alphabet a couple of times beforehand if you have not done so recently. Bon voyage!

WELCOME ABOARD!

With *Captain Bucko's Nauti-Words Handbook* in your sea bag or on your bookshelf, you will be able to amaze friends and confound enemies with your nautical knowledge. Landlubbers, sea lawyers, blow-boaters, stink-potters, pollywogs, and even shellbacks are very likely to learn interesting facts (and fables) about the origins of everyday expressions and nautical terms like garboard and lagan.

(Picture Courtesy of the Naval Historical Center)

Now let's cast off and get underway…and stand by to be amazed!

A

A1—This synonym for being first-class came from a rating given wooden ships in *Lloyd's Register*[1], with the letter "A" referring to the quality of their hulls and the number "1" referring to the quality of their equipment. It is also the name of a brand of steak sauce, but that is another story.

Abaft—For some reason, landlubbers get confused about the proper use of nautical terms that pertain to location and direction, but as you will discover, there is a key to many of them. This is the first such a term, and it is used to describe something located aft (sternward) of something else, e.g., "Her poop deck is abaft her mast." (Also see Aft, Astern, Landlubber, Mast, and Poop Deck.)

Abandon Ship!—Because this is the order given to leave a burning, sinking, or otherwise seriously troubled vessel, you might want to remember it. It just could come in quite handy someday.

Abeam—Besides describing what comes out of the end of a flashlight, this nautical term is used to denote a location that is directly off a vessel's beam. This is the second term that pertains to a location or to a direction, so a-have a-you a-discovered a-the a-key a-yet? (Also see Beam.)

Able-Bodied Seaman—Sometimes abbreviated as "AB," this phrase was used to describe an individual who could perform all of the duties of an experienced mariner, was certificated by examination, and had at least three years of service at sea. (Also see Mariner and Ordinary Seaman.)

---

1.   Lloyd's Register is an independent risk management organization founded in 1760 to examine and classify merchant vessels according to their condition.

Aboard—This term evolved from earlier times when the planks that made up vessels' hulls were called "boards," for fairly obvious reasons. It is used to refer to things or persons who are in, or on, vessels. *Trivial Tidbit*—Members of a ship's company are considered to be "in" a vessel, while individuals who are along for the ride e.g., passengers, are "on" her. Captain Bucko included this trivial tidbit so that you would not become…ah, bored. (Also see Board and Ship's Company.)

A Bone In Her Teeth—This strange phrase does not describe a female cannibal, but rather the condition that occurs when spray and foam are thrown aside from beneath the bow of a fast moving vessel. (Also see Bow.)

Above Board—This phrase was originally used to describe items on or above a vessel's open decks, and came from days when pirate ships often hid most of their crews below deck. These days we use the phrase to mean something that is in plain view, or someone who is honest and open. (Also see Below Deck, Deck, and Pirate.)

A Cat Has Nine Lives—This expression can be traced back to the infamous "cat o' nine tails," which could inflict pain until the very last of its nine flails was lost. (Also see Cat O' Nine Tails.)

Accommodation Ladder—This is the term for a folding ladder often used to transfer between pilot boats and larger vessels, etc. For more excitement, use the Jacob's Ladder. (Also see Jacob's Ladder.)

A Couple Of Shakes—These days we use this phrase to mean "in a few seconds," but it originally referred to shaking of the sails if a vessel was headed too close into the wind. This may occur as a helmsman's attention lapsed near the end of their watch, so sailors began to describe the short time periods before a vessel's watch changes as "a couple of shakes."

Adrift—This nautical term is used to denote objects that are not under control, but are floating free with the winds and currents. This same term can also be properly applied to certain individuals.

Admiral—In the 12th Century Moslem fleets were some of the most formidable in the Mediterranean, and this word evolved from the Arabic term *amir-al-bahr*, their title for a fleet commander. Today, it denotes a senior flag officer in the US Navy or US Coast Guard.

Aft—This nautical term denotes being toward, near, or at a vessel's stern. *Handy Hint*—If you are aboard a vessel that is moving ahead and the objects on shore appear to be getting smaller, there is an excellent chance that either: (1) you are facing aft, or (2) those objects really ARE decreasing in size. And by the way, aft is the opposite of the term "forward." (Also see Forward.)

Aground—This term refers to a vessel that is touching, or fast on the bottom. Most of us do not like to run aground on a regular basis, but sometimes grounding can be intentional. Foundering vessels may be grounded in an attempt to save lives or cargo, and prior to dry docks ships were sometimes (gently) grounded to perform hull maintenance or repairs. On December 7, 1941, the USS Nevada was grounded to prevent her from sinking in the entrance to

Pearl Harbor. Amphibious assault craft are often intentionally grounded, and as part of his sales pitch to sell landing craft to the US Navy, Mr. Andrew Jackson Higgins sometimes parked one of his boats upon Lake Ponchartrain's seawall. This must have worked, because at the height of World War II over 90% of the Navy's boats used one of Higgins' designs. (Also see Boat, Careen, Fast, and Hard Aground.)

Ahead—Since the term "head" is also used to refer to a vessel's forward end, you may not be very surprised to learn this nautical term refers to that direction, e.g., "Full Speed Ahead!" (Also see Forward and Head.)

Ahoy!—This was once a battle cry of the feared Vikings, but after they cut way back on their pillaging it became a common greeting among other mariners. (Also see Mariner.)

Aids To Navigation—This phrase refers to fixed or floating objects like lighthouses, markers, buoys, etc. These can come in quite handy for determining just how far off course you actually are!

All Arms And Legs—We sometimes use this to describe a teenager whose body parts seem to be growing at different rates, but it once referred to a vessel that was carrying too much sail.

All Hands On Deck!—This command was originally, "All Hands Hoay!" It means that everyone should muster on their station and prepare for action. We still use this nautical phrase to gather people for some task or project.

All Sewn Up—Today we use this phrase to denote that something is complete, but it actually came from those buried at sea being "all sewn up" in sail canvas or in hammocks with weights to ensure they sank. The sewing began at their feet, with the last stitch being taken through their noses (just to make sure that they were really dead.) Although records are sketchy, most think this probably worked! (Also see Hammocks.)

All Washed Up—If their vessel ran aground, mariners could find themselves left ashore without any means of support. This originally referred to someone in such a predicament, but today it is used to denote somebody who is a has-been. (Also see Aground and Mariner.)

Aloof—Some say that this word evolved from the Dutch term for windward, and was used to describe vessels that stayed upwind and away from the rest of the fleet. Others suggest it came from the phrase "all off," as in to stand off a dangerous shore. In any case, we currently use the term "aloof" to mean somebody who is snobbish, distant, or stands apart. (Also see Windward.)

Amidships—Here is still another nautical location term! This one is used to denote a location that is at, or near, the center of a vessel's length and/or breadth. (Also see Centerline and Waist.)

Any Port In A Storm—The meaning of this old saying has not changed much over the years. If a vessel or person is in serious difficulty, they are likely to seek safety and help almost anywhere.

Armed To The Teeth—The origin of this phrase is uncertain, but maybe it came from all those pictures we have seen of pirates with cutlasses in their mouths…or maybe not. (Also see Cutlass and Pirate.)

Astern—This nautical tern is used to describe things that are in the direction of a vessel's stern. Astern is the opposite of the term "ahead." A-hem, do you see any pattern here yet? (Also see Ahead and Stern.)

As The Crow Flies—Early mariners sometimes carried crows or ravens (similar to crows on steroids) aboard their vessels. When uncertain of their position in coastal waters, they would release a bird that usually flew directly toward the nearest land. Now days, this phrase is often used to describe a direct route to someplace. (Also see Crow's Nest and Mariner.)

A Stitch In Time Saves Nine—This very common expression came from the days when sail-maker's assistants were required to use at least nine stitches per inch. If they did not, the sail-maker would rip all of their stitches out and make them try again. Worse, for every inch with fewer than nine stitches, they would receive nine strokes from the cat o' nine tails. (Also see Cat O' Nine Tails.)

Athwartships—This rather salty-sounding term simply refers to being perpendicular to a vessel's centerline, as opposed to being oriented fore-and aft. (Also see Centerline and Fore-And-Aft).

At Loggerheads—This phrase originated in the days when small arms, e.g., cutlasses, pistols, were tightly controlled on board most vessels for a number of reasons. A loggerhead was the name for an iron ball on a long handle. Such balls were heated and used to melt the tar (a distillate of pine pitch) for sealing a vessel's seams and tarring her rigging. When crewmen were "at loggerheads," it meant that their quarrel had escalated to physical violence. This phrase still refers to an impasse.

At Loose Ends—Now days we tie up loose ends to finally settle a matter, but this phrase originally referred to an unattached or neglected rope that was not doing its job. (Also see Line and Rope.)

Avast!—Contrary to what other sources might say, a "vast" is quite different from a "hoy." Actually, this nautical command means to halt an action, e.g., "Avast me hearties!" (Also see Belay.)

Aweigh—This nautical term actually means to hoist an anchor off of the bottom. It does not mean to bring an anchor completely on board, as many people think. (Also see Aboard and Weigh.)

Aye, Aye—Aye is simply the old English word for "yes." In nautical terms, "Aye, aye, sir!" means that one understands and will comply with an order. If one chooses not to do so, also see Mutiny.

B

Baboon Watch—This is the nautical phrase for standing watch aboard a vessel in port, while others in the ship's company went ashore on liberty or relaxed onboard. This duty was typically given to a vessel's newest crewmember, since real baboons were much more difficult to find than sailors in most ports. (Also see Ship's Company.)

Backing and Filling—These days this is used to describe the actions of someone who is indecisive, and frequently changes positions on decisions or arguments. It originally meant to let the sails alternately draw then spill wind, so that a vessel would (more or less) mark time and remain in one place.

Bad Luck Friday—Mariners tend to be a bit superstitious, and some are very reluctant to set sail on a Friday. To discredit this superstition, the British government supposedly once laid the keel of a new vessel on a Friday, launched her on a Friday, named her the HMS Friday, gave her to a Captain Friday, and sent her on her maiden voyage on a Friday. All seemed to be going quite well, except that she was never heard from again.

Bail—This nautical term refers to either: (1) removing water from a vessel with a bucket, pump, etc., or (2) an iron rod to which a sheet block is attached. *Helpful Hint*—When sinking, the former definition should take precedence over the latter. (Also see Sheet.)

Ballast—This nautical term refers to heavy materials like iron, stones, gravel, etc. that are placed low within a vessel's hull and/or keel to increase stability, provide proper trim, improve her sea-keeping ability, and/or submerge her propeller. In early sailing ships river rocks were often used as ballast, while in many modern vessels water may be pumped into onboard ballast tanks. (Also see Keel.)

Balls To The Wall—This originally referred to the design of early mechanical engine governors that spun metal balls in a growing circle as the engine speed increased. The phrase, "balls to the wall" was simply used to denote maximum speed. But that was what you were already thinking, right?

Bamboozle—When this term was first used it referred to the serious, and sometimes deadly, practice of deceiving other vessels by flying colors (flags) other than one's own. This was a common tactic of pirates, and was also used by the Spanish to bamboozle enemies. (Also see Showing One's True Colors.)

Barque—(pronounced *bark.*) This is the nautical term for a sailing vessel with three to five masts and square rigging upon all except her aftermost mast, which is rigged fore-and-aft. The traditional three-mast versions were common deep-

Barque

water cargo vessels in the mid-1800s, but steel-hulled ones with four or more masts began to appear in the early 20th Century. The US Coast Guard's training ship *Eagle* is a Barque. (Also see Fore-And-Aft and Mast.) (Figure Courtesy of J. Wilkinson)

Barquentine—(pronounced *bark-en-teen.*) You could use this term for a teenager who thinks he or she is a dog, but it actually refers to a schooner that has at least three-masts and is square-rigged only on her foremast. Three-mast versions of these ships were quite

Barquentine

common in the North and Baltic Seas, and along with Barquentines having four or more masts, were used for deep-water trading. (Also see Mast and Schooner.) (Figure Courtesy of J. Wilkinson)

Bar Shot—This does not necessarily refer of a glass of sprits, but also to a type of early cannon projectile in a dumbbell shape that was fired into an enemy's rigging to cut their lines and sails.

Batten—This term is used to mean either: (1) a short piece of wood or plastic that may be inserted into a sail, or (2) a thin strip of wood that is placed around hatches to hold down tarpaulins or onto rigging to prevent chafing. (Also see Batten Down and Tarpaulin.)

Batten Down—This phrase could refer to either: (1) fitting thin wood strips around the coamings of ladder ways and hatchways to hold tarpaulins down in foul weather, or (2) securing hatches and loose objects in the hull or on deck. It is not the opposite of, "Batter up!" (Also see Coaming, Deck, Hatch, Secure, and Tarpaulin.)

Beachcomber—Long before this meant somebody who gathers seashells and driftwood, it was used for a derelict seaman who hung about a port and lived on others' charity. It is still used to describe a waterfront loafer who prefers not to work. Another idyllic image gets destroyed!

Beakhead—This is the nautical term for the pointed ram upon the prow of a war galley. It was designed to pierce the hulls of enemy vessels. (Also see Galley, Head, and Prow.)

Beam—This nautical term may be used to describe: (1) the breadth of a vessel at her widest point, and (2) a transverse member of a vessel's frame upon which her deck planks are laid. (Also see Abeam, Deck, and Planking.)

Beam Ends—If a vessel lies over so far that her deck beams are nearly vertical, she is said to be, "on her beam ends." Before dry-docks, this was sometimes done intentionally as a way to perform hull repairs or maintenance. (Also see Careen and Deck.)

Bearing—This term refers to the direction of something from the observer's location, and is also used to describe that part of a vessel's hull on her waterline when she is at anchor and in proper trim…but we must not neglect to also mention those ball and roller bearings! (Also see Waterline.)

Beating The Booby—This rather colorful nautical phrase actually refers to warming your hands in your armpits. You look a bit like a booby bird (an Albatross), which many regard as cerebrally challenged.

Becalm—This means to intercept the wind. A high coastline, or even another vessel to windward, can becalm one's vessel. Becalming works much better on sailing vessels, however. (Also see Windward.)

Before The Mast—Perhaps you have been curious about that old saying, "He sailed before the mast"…or perhaps not. It comes from the fact that unlicensed crewmen's living quarters were often in their vessel's forecastle, which was forward of her foremast. On the other hand, officers usually lived more aft in early sailing vessels. (Also see Aft, Forecastle, Foremast, and Forward.)

Belay—This nautical term is used to mean: (1) to make a line fast by turning it around a cleat, etc., and (2) to stop or cancel something, e.g., "Belay that!" (Also see Avast, Cleat, Fast, and Line.)

Bell Bottom Trousers—These wide flared legs apparently were first introduced in the early 1800s, and they had practical values. It was easier for sailors to roll up their trouser legs when in partially flooded spaces or while swabbing decks, and to remove their trousers over their footwear if they ever found themselves on the "wrong side" of their vessel's hull.

Below Deck—This nautical phrase refers to being under a vessel's deck or in her cabin. This term may sometimes be abbreviated to "below," e.g., "I am going below now." (Also see Cabin and Deck.)

Bend—This nautical term is used to mean: (1) a knot by which one line is made fast to another, and (2) to make something fast, e.g., bend a line to a cleat. (Also see Cleat, Fast, and Line.)

Berth—This nautical term is commonly used to refer to a place where: (1) a vessel lies, (2) a person sleeps, or (3) both.

Between The Devil And The Deep—This odd phrase stems from the unpopular, but periodically necessary, task of caulking a wooden vessel's "devil" seams. One of them was the longest seam that ran from bow to stern and quite close to the side. Others included those seams close to or slightly below the waterline that could only be caulked when the vessel was on her beam ends, careened, or heeled over while underway. Lashed about their feet or waists, crewmen would be dangled over the side to do this job. They often got caught by waves or submerged completely if the vessel rolled in their direction, and would be flogged if they lost any gear overboard. We still use this phrase to describe being in an unenviable position. (Also see Beam Ends, Bow, Careen, Stern, Underway, and Waterline.)

Bight—This nautical term is used for: (1) any part of a rope or line except its ends, very commonly the doubled (loop) portion if it is folded, and (2) an indentation in a shoreline that forms a small inlet, cove, bay, etc....just try not to bight anybody! (Also see Line and Rope.)

Bigwigs—Once senior officers in the British Navy wore huge wigs, and were irreverently called "bigwigs." Now days it is used for individuals who (think they) are very important persons.

Bilge—This nautical term may refer to either: (1) the lowest part within a vessel's hull below the waterline and near her keel, or (2) the largest circumference of a cask or barrel. (Also see Keel and Waterline.)

Bilge Pump—This refers to an electrically, mechanically, or manually operated device used to remove water from a vessel's bilge. If you do not have a good one, get two! (Also see Bilge.)

Bilge Water—This nautical phrase refers to the water and other interesting things that settle in a vessel's bilge. It is also a phrase used to mean something of dubious veracity. (Also see Bilge.)

Binge—This word came from the old nautical term for rinsing or cleaning out something. A sailor (or a college student) who has "cleaned out" a keg of beer is said to have binged.

Binnacle—This is the nautical term for the fixture near the helm that houses a vessel's compass, etc.

Binnacle List—This is the term for a vessel's sick list. A listing of crewmembers unable to stand duty was provided to the mate or the officer of the watch and kept by the binnacle. (Also see Binnacle, Mate, and Officer.)

Bird's Nest—This term is used to mean: (1) a small round platform situated precariously higher on a vessel 's mast than a crow's nest to enable lookouts to see greater distances, and (2) a tangled mess of line that is a common occurrence among new boaters, landlubbers, etc. (Also see Crow's Nest, Landlubber, Line, and Mast.)

Bitter End—This currently means sticking with something or someone until nothing else can be done, but it originated aboard vessels where lines are secured to "bitts." When all of a line or chain has been paid out, it is said to have come to its "bitter end." This term was also used for a "starter," which was a short, knotted line that was used for…crew motivation. (Also see Line.)

Black Book—If you offend somebody you might be listed in their black book, a phrase that goes all the way back to the 1300s when a collection of maritime rules of conduct and laws called the *Black Book of the Admiralty* came out. Some of the punishments that it suggested included marooning, starvation, and drowning, all of which were real morale boosters for sailors.

Black Jack—Before this became a casino game, mariners used this term for: (1) the bubonic plague, which was said to turn its victims black, (2) a leather tankard stiffened with a coating of tar that was sometimes used by waterfront taverns to serve beer and wine, and (3) a flag flown by pirates. Edward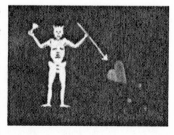
Teach, who was more commonly known as Blackbeard, once flew the flag shown here. (Also see Jolly Roger, Pirate, and Skull And Cross Bones.)

Blazers—Although uniforms for low-rated personnel were not at all common, some Captains liked to show off their crews during ceremonial events. Their blue jackets were so memorable that the crewmen of the HMS Blazer became known as "Blazers," and the garment became standard attire around many yacht clubs.

Blood Is Thicker Than Water—This saying goes back to Navy Commodore Josiah Tattnail, who used it to justify his coming to the rescue of the British during the second China war.

Blood Money—This phrase originally referred to the financial reward that was given for the sinking of enemy vessels and was based upon the number of her crewmen killed…not upon the sunken vessels' size or importance.

Blooper—Apologies to Dick Clark and Ed McMahon, but this nautical term refers to a lightweight foresail that is quite similar to a spinnaker except that it is set without a pole. (Also see Spinnaker.)

Blow-boater—This is one of the (more respectful) terms that power-boaters often use for an individual who prefers sailing vessels…especially when they are clogging up a very narrow channel by making aberrant and entirely too frequent course changes. (Also see Tack, Stinkpotter, and Windjammer.)

Blowhard—Some say that this nautical word could be the literal translation of the landlubber's term "politician." (Also see Landlubber.)

Blowing The Grampus—Of course by now you realize that this is the nautical phrase for waking up a sailor who is asleep on watch by throwing a bucket of cold water upon them. However, these days it seems to be more common in football stadiums.

Blow The Man Down—Most think that the title to this famous sea chantey actually means "knock the man down," and some maintain it was derived from an African-American ditty called "Knock A Man Down." The lyrics indicate that it pertains to the American's Black Ball Line, which was well known for fast packet ships and brutality to their crews. The Chief Mates aboard the Western Ocean ships were known as "blowers" in those days, so this might refer to one of them knocking a sailor to the deck. (Also see Chantey, Deck, and Mate.)

Blue Monday—If you believe that Mondays are tough for you, consider that this phrase originated because aboard early ships Monday was often punishment day for their crews. (Also see Crew.)

Blue Peter—This nautical phrase refers to the signal flag for the letter "P," which is flown to indicate that all should report aboard because a vessel is about to depart. All aboard!

Board—Depending upon the context, this term could mean: (1) the planks making up the vessel's hull, (2) to come aboard (embark in) a vessel, or (3) a common piece of lumber. (Also see Aboard, Board And Board, By The Boards, Embark, Larboard, Overboard, Outboard, Planking, and Starboard [Side].)

Board And Board—This is the nautical phrase used to describe vessels lying so close side-to-side that they almost touch each other. (Also see Close Aboard and Yardarm And Yardarm.)

Boat—This is a generic term for a small vessel that might be propelled by oars, sail, paddles, or an engine. It comes from the Anglo-Saxon word *bat*, which simply meant a small vessel.

Boatswain—(pronounced *bo'-sun*.) This was originally a title for an individual responsible for one of several types of boats that all Royal Navy warships were required to carry. Over time it evolved into meaning the person responsible for deck hands and equipment, as well as the sails, rigging, lines, piping the crew, boats, meting out punishment, etc. (Also see Boat, Boatswain's Pipe, Combing The Cat, Crew, and Line.)

Boatswain's Chair—This is the nautical term for a plank seat or a canvas sling often used to hoist crewmembers so they could maintain or repair a vessel's sails, rigging, etc.

Boatswain's Locker—This nautical term refers to a vessel's onboard storage space(s) for tools, supplies, etc.

Boatswain's Pipe—The Greeks and Romans used a version of such a pipe-shaped whistle to meter the oar strokes of their war galleys. Another version was used during the Crusades to call English crossbowmen on deck for battle. It is the boatswain's badge of office, and it is equivalent to a bugle in the cavalry. The Boatswain's Pipe is used today for rendering honors, etc. (Also see Boatswain, Deck, and Galley.)

Booby Hatch—This phrase evolved into meaning a mental institution, but originally it referred to the opening of a small forward compartment where crewmembers were sometimes confined as punishment for relatively minor offenses. Hey, it still sounds like a lot more fun than flogging or keelhauling! (Also see Cat O' Nine Tails, Forward, and Keelhauling.)

Boot Camp—During the Spanish-American War, sailors wore leggings more commonly called boots. "Boots" also became a nickname for Navy recruits, who to this very day still train in Boot Camps.

Booty—Regardless of what this means to you today or how well you shake it, this once referred to the goods from captured ships that were quickly distributed among their captors.

Born With a Silver Spoon—This phrase was originally used for men who, through their birthright or connections, were allowed to join the Royal Navy without examination, and for whom subsequent promotions were all but assured. Some things never change!

Bow—This is the nautical term for the forward part of the vessel (usually the pointy end). If you are confused, just stand facing the stern—the bow should be behind you. (Also see Forward and Stern.)

Bow Line—This phrase refers to a line that leads from a vessel's bow laterally to a dock, etc. This line's primary function is to keep the vessel's bow alongside the dock. (Also see Bow, Dock, and Line.)

Bowline—(pronounced bo'-lin) This famous nautical knot is simple, yet strong and slip-proof. It is often used to make a loop or an eye in a line, and can be untied easily even after it has been under a strain. (Also see Line.)

Bowsprit—(pronounced *bo-sprit*) This is the nautical term for a large, strong spar that stands out from a sailing vessel's bow. It is used to support the masts and to carry sails. So many crewmen died while working in the area, the bowsprit was nicknamed the "widow maker." (Also see Bow, Mast, Spar, and Widow Maker.)

Bow Thruster—This relatively new term refers to a small propeller or impeller mounted below the waterline in the bow, for skippers who just can't get the knack of docking. (Also see Bow, Dock, Skipper, and Waterline.)

Boxing The Compass—This phrase originally referred to being able to recite all the points of the compass in both clockwise and counter-clockwise directions, but today it is often used to describe a person who uses circular logic and ends up just about where they started.

Brace Up—These days we may say, "Come on, brace up!" as encouragement, but this term originally meant to tighten the ship's rigging. So brace up, things could get worse at sea!

Breast Line—This is the nautical term for a line that may be attached laterally amidships to prevent a vessel's movement away from a dock, etc. (Also see, Amidships, Dock, and Line.)

Breeches Buoy—This is the name for a device sometimes used to rescue persons from wrecked or vessels in distress. It might be fired onto such a vessel's deck by a cannon. (Also see Deck.)

Bridge—This is the nautical term for the location from which larger vessels are controlled. It is equivalent to a "control station" found aboard a smaller craft.

Brig—In addition to being the term used for a Navy jail, this refers to a two-mast vessel that has square-rigged sails on both masts plus a gaff sail on her aftermost mast. In some locales, the latter sail is also known as a *brig sail* or a *spanker*. Some Brigs might even have

Brig

such sails on a separate mast just *aft* of their main masts. Such separate masts were known as *snow masts*, and such vessels were often called *Snow Brigs*. Brigs were well known for their maneuverability, and in the hands of skilled Masters they were said to be able to turn on a doubloon (there very few dimes back then). (Also see Aft, Doubloon, Mast, Main Mast, and Master.) (Figure Courtesy of J. Wilkinson)

Brigantine—Some say this term originally was used for any vessel manned by brigands, but it actually refers to two-mast schooners having square-rigged foremasts and main masts with a fore-and-aft mainsail (and possibly also square-rigged topsails). This describes traditional Brigantines, while vessels

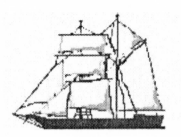

Brigantine

without any square-rigged sails upon their main masts were actually called *Hermaphrodite Brigs*. (Also see Brig, Fore-And-Aft, Main Mast, Mainsail, and Schooner.) (Figure Courtesy of J. Wilkinson)

Broach—In addition to being a ladies' pin, this nautical term refers to the swinging or turning of a vessel in such a way that it puts the seas upon her beam, resulting in a loss of control and a serious risk of swamping or capsizing. (Also see Beam.)

Broadside—This nautical term is used to refer to: (1) the entire side of a vessel, and (2) the firing of all the guns on one side of a vessel simultaneously.

Brought Before The Mast—This refers to a crewmember being brought before the vessel's Captain on disciplinary charges. Would you care to guess where this was done aboard ship? (Also see Captain.)

Brought Up Short—Today we use this for someone who has been interrupted by an unforeseen event, but it also refers to stopping a vessel by dropping her anchors.

Buccaneer—This term has a somewhat convoluted origin. The French referred to early natives of the West Indies as *bou-caniers,* for the way that they roasted and smoked meat in a pit called a *boucan.* By the 17th Century however, a number of runaway slaves, criminals, and other refugees who had a particular dislike for Spaniards had gathered in the Caribbean. Some of them operated as privateers like Henry Morgan, who was known as much for his ruthless nature as for his skills in

Ol' Hank Morgan

battle. They became known as Buccaneers, which is a long way from being known as a piece of smoked meat! (Also see Privateer.)

Bucko—This is the nickname given a tyrannical officer who drove the crew through brutality and intimidation. However, Captain Bucko has found this technique to be quite effective.

Bulkhead—This nautical term refers to a vertical partition that divides a vessel's interior into compartments. While they are not necessarily watertight, bulkheads may contain damages.

Bully Boys—A staple in the diet of sailors in the colonial Navy was a sort of jerky called "salt junk," or "bully beef." It was so common that it became the basis for this nickname for the sailors who had to eat it. (Also see Chewing The Fat.)

Bulwark—This is a nautical term for that part of a vessel's side that extends above her main deck: for protection in heavy weather, to prevent things and people from being lost overboard, and to keep (most of) the water on the proper side of her hull. (Also see Main Deck and Overboard.)

Bum Boat—Probably derived from a Dutch word for a broad-beamed boat, this became the term for any boat that comes alongside vessels in port selling provisions, souvenirs, or to remove trash. However, it could also refer to a small craft that is full of vagrants, hobos, etc.

Bumboo—This odd word refers to the mixture of water, rum, sugar, and nutmeg that was a popular drink among pirates, buccaneers, and West Indies natives. (Also see Buccaneer and Pirate.)

Bung Up And Bilge Free—This is the rather complex nautical phrase for "OK." So why didn't you just say that, Okay?

Bunkering—This nautical term simply refers to the process of refueling a vessel. Try using it the next time you pull up to your local fuel pier, and see what happens!

Buoyed Up—We use this phrase to denote encouragement, but it originally referred to using a buoy to lift the bight of an anchor rode to keep it from chafing on the bottom. (Also see Bight and Rode.)

Burdened Vessel—This refers to a vessel that, in accordance with applicable navigational Rules of the Road, should give way to a privileged vessel. (Also see Give-Way Vessel, Privileged Vessel, and Rules Of The Road.)

Burgee—This is the nautical term for a type of flag that is often used to identify affiliation with a yacht club or a boating organization. "Don't forget to fly that cute little burgee of yours, dear!"

Burgoo—This name for a 17th century gruel made from grain and seasoned with sugar, salt, and butter came from the Hindu term *bar-goo* meaning "feces of the sacred cow." Sounds yummy, doesn't it?

Burning One's Boats—We use this phrase to mean cutting off all means of retreat, leaving no way back. For example, after the mutineers got to Pitcairn Island they purposely burned the HMS Bounty.

By And Large—This phrase was derived from combining the two nautical terms "by" meaning *into* the wind, and "large" meaning *with* the wind. It is used to describe the ability to do something reasonably well under various conditions.

By The Boards—Today this phrase describes a lost opportunity or letting something pass, but it originally referred to the planking on a vessel's sides. When an object was seen to go over the vessels' side or passing by in the water, it was said to have gone "by the boards." (Also see Overboard and Planking.)

C

Cabin—This nautical term refers an enclosed compartment within a vessel that is typically used as either a shelter or as living quarters for her passengers and/or her crewmembers.

Caboose—Some maintain this term actually came from the old nautical term "camboose," which originally referred to a large wood stove or to a small enclosure on deck where cooking was done. It was the only place that a large fire was allowed onboard, and might be also used as a forge. After sailors began to use the term "galley," they generously let the railroaders use the term "caboose." (Also see Deck and Galley.)

Cackle Fruit—Sailing vessels sometimes carried chickens, goats, or other livestock aboard during length voyages. The goats provided milk, and this was the nautical term for the hens' eggs.

Cad—This term is currently used for a boorish person, but it came from the "cad's corner," that section of a wardroom's table where the young and more exuberant could be caddish. (Also see Wardroom.)

Camel—In nautical jargon, this term is used for both: (1) a float placed between a vessel and a dock, and (2) a hollow device that was filled with water and sunk beneath a vessel, then pumped out to help lift her over shallow water areas. (Also see Dock.)

Canteen Medal—This is a sailor's picturesque phrase for a food or drink stain upon the front of one's jumper, coat, etc.

Caper—This term originally did not have anything to do with crime. Instead, it was the nickname used for a fisherman from Cape Clear, Ireland, who was said to go out in the fiercest weather.

Capstan—This is the term for a spool-shaped, mechanical device that is mounted vertically on a vessel's deck and used for the hoisting of anchors, sails, and other very heavy objects.

Captain—Technically the rank of Captain is a military title, while the licensed head of a non-military vessel is a Master. Those operating a vessel without a Master's License should not be addressed as Captain, but it has become acceptable to call the licensed Master of a commercial or pleasure craft "Captain." When in doubt use "Skipper," just like Gilligan did. (Also see Master and Skipper.)

Captain Of The Heads—This was the unenviable title given to the crewmember given the job of cleaning a vessel's sanitary facilities. Hey, they made me a Captain! (Also see Captain and Head.)

Caravel—These were relatively small and lightweight three-mast trading vessels that were (typically) square-rigged upon their two forward masts, and lateen-rigged upon their mizzenmasts. Caravels (or Carvels) were developed by the Portuguese in the late 15th Century to help them discover a way around Africa to the Far East, but these merchant vessels became quite popular for explorations over the next 300 years. The *Nina* and the *Pinta* used by Columbus were Caravels, as well as the vessels that were used by some guy named Magellan. (Also see Lateen, Mast, and Mizzenmast.)

Careen—If the hull of a large wooden vessel had to be patched, caulked, cleaned, etc., it might be "careened" by deliberately leaning the vessel over onto her side. This was usually done when the tide was out over a steep, sandy shore that was called a *careenage*. These days we still use this term to describe something that leans over wildly. (Also see Beam Ends.)

Carrack—This was another three-mast trading vessel that was square-rigged on her fore and main mast, lateen-rigged on her mizzenmast, but larger than a Caravel. The Tudor era Carracks had tall masts with huge sails, deep round hulls, and high forecastles. (Also see Caravel, Forecastle, Foremast, Lateen, Mast, Main Mast, and Mizzenmast.)

Carrick Bend—This is the name of another nautical knot that is often used to join two lines together. (Also see Line.)

Carry Away—Before getting too "carried away," you should know that this nautical phrase means to break something off or to part a line. At sea, it might be literally carried away. (Also see Line.)

Carry On!—These days this phrase means to resume work, but in the old days it was the command given to unfurl all the sails when a good wind came along. Or a Mate might say, "Carry On!" to cool tempers if a fight appeared imminent among the crewmembers. (Also see At Loggerheads, Mate, and Unfurl.)

Cast Adrift—This refers to putting people into a boat or onto a raft, and abandoning them at sea. (Also see Boat, Castaway, and Marooned.)

Castaway—There is a subtle, yet important, difference between a castaway (a shipwrecked person) and somebody who has been marooned ashore as a punishment. (Also see Marooned.)

Cast Off!—This nautical command means to release a vessel's mooring lines or her sheets. (Also see Line, Mooring, and Sheet.)

Catboat—This is not what you are probably thinking! It is simply a nautical term for a sailboat that has one mast and one sail. (Also see Mast and Sailboat.)

Catch My Drift—Like this nautical term like means like do you like know what I like mean and like know where I'm coming from, Dude?

Catenary—This term refers to the sag in a line, cable, or chain that is strung between two points. It can be an important factor for absorbing shocks and anchoring vessels securely. (Also see Line.)

Cathead—This is the nautical term for a heavy timber that projects from a vessel's bow and is used to secure, or "cat," her anchor after it is weighed or prior to letting it go. (Also see Bow.)

Cat O' Nine Tails—This was a whip with nine separate flails, attached to a handle, and used to flog adult sailors. *Trivial Tidbit*—There was also a lesser version with five flails that was used for flogging younger crewmembers. (Also see Combing The Cat, Let The Cat Out Of The Bag, Over The Barrel, and Pussy Whipped.)

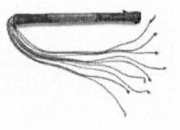

Cat's Paw—This nautical term may mean: (1) a ripple that is caused by a light breath of air on an otherwise calm water surface, and (2) a hitch that is used to form two eyes in a line. (Also see Line.)

Catwalk—This term for a narrow, raised passageway originated back when some of the later sailing vessels and early steamships were equipped with such a walkway to connect elevated structures such as: forecastles, bridges, and poop decks. Although they offered drier and safer paths, one frequently had to be as agile as a cat to traverse them during very heavy weather. (Also see Bridge, Forecastle, and Poop Deck.)

Caulking—This is a general term for: (1) materials used to make the seams in a vessel watertight, and (2) the actual process of making a vessel's seams watertight. Watertight is a good thing!

Ceiling—This is an acceptable nautical term for a vessel's interior horizontal planking. (Also see Overhead.)

Centerboard—This is the term for an often removable, fin-shaped board that extends from the bottom of a sailboat and serves as a keel to reduce sideward motion. (Also see Keel and Sailboat.)

Centerline—This term refers to a hypothetical line that runs down the center of a vessel from her bow to her stern. A vessel's centerline length is a very common dimensional specification.

Chafing Gear—This is the general term for devices used to prevent or reduce the effects of one object rubbing against another. Using such a definition, were chastity belts a medieval type of chafing gear?

Chain Locker—This refers to the space(s) in the bow, and possibly also the vessel's stern, used to stow her anchor chain(s). These spaces are often located low within the hull, because chains are heavy. (Also see Bow and Stern.)

Chain Shot—This was a type of projectile that consisted of two cannon-balls connected by a short length of chain, and designed to destroy the rigging of enemy vessels. *Trivial Tidbit*—There was another variation called "Angel Shot," that consisted of two cannon ball halves joined by a similar piece of chain.

Chandlery—Today this term is most often used for a store that sells nautical supplies, but it is also a name for a place where candles are made and sold. This commonality exists because until whale oil became more readily available in the early 1700s, vessels used large quantities of candles for illumination. Every port call meant a visit to a local chandlery to replenish the supply of candles, until enterprising chandlers began to stock other nautical items as well. Good thing too, since today marine supplies tend to outsell candles by quite a bit.

Chantey—(also spelled *chanty, shanty, etc.*) These were work songs used aboard ships. Their various rhythms were used to coordinate the crew's manual efforts and pace different types of tasks, e.g., hauling on lines. (Also see Crew and Line.)

Charlie Noble—Believe it or not, this is a nautical phrase for the smokestack of a vessel's galley. Its namesake apparently was a real person who took great pride in keeping such a pipe shiny. (Also see Galley.)

Cheese Down—This nautical phrase means to coil a line so as to present a neat appearance. It is not a football term from the University of Wisconsin! (Also see Coil and Line.)

Cheerily!—This was the old nautical command that meant to do something quickly and with vigor. So let's keelhaul him, cheerily!

Chewing The Fat—During the 19th century, salted meat was a staple aboard ship. It was quite common on longer voyages when nothing else was as cheap or kept as well without refrigeration. Since it needed prolonged mastication to be edible, passengers sometimes thought that the sailors looked like they were always sitting around talking. When they asked the Master what the crewmen were doing, he might just say, "chewing the fat." These days, we use the same phrase to describe friendly conversations. Blah, blah, blah, blah...(Also see Bully Boys and Master.)

Chine—This is the term used for the place(s) where the sides and the bottom of a vessel intersect. There are hard chines, soft chines, and reverse chines, so feel free to just "chine in" anytime!

Chit—This Navy term for a promissory note stems back to the days when Hindu traders used slips of paper called *chitthi*, so they did not have to carry around heavy bags of silver or gold. British sailors adapted the term for their mess vouchers, and shortened the word to "chit." The term is still used in today's navies for leave, liberty, and other special request forms. (Also see Mess.)

Chock-A-Block—These days this is used to mean that things (or persons) are packed tightly together or something that is filled to capacity, but it originally meant that two blocks of a vessel's rigging tackle were together so firmly they could not be tightened any further. (Also see Hard Up and Tackle.)

Clean Bill of Health—This phrase evolved from the days when "Bill of Health" documents were issued to vessels, certifying that the ports from which they came suffered no contagious diseases or epidemics, and that no crewmembers were infected with such diseases at the time of that vessel's departure.

Clean Slate—In the early days of sail, watch keepers recorded their vessel's speeds, distances, headings, and tacks on a slate tablet that was kept close by the helm. If there were no problems, it would be wiped clean so the oncoming watch could "start with a clean slate." Today we use this same phrase to denote a fresh start, a new beginning, etc. (Also see Heading, Tack, and Watches.)

Clear The Deck!—These days we use this phrase when we are preparing to start something, but it originally was the order given to get ready for foul weather or a battle by removing all non-essential objects from the deck so that they would not become hazards or interfere with the crew's activities.

Cleat—This is the nautical term for a fitting with two horns about which lines can be made fast. Cleats may be mounted on docks, pilings, vessels' decks, etc. (Also see Deck, Dock, Fast, and Line.)

Clipper Ship—This was a generic term used for the sailing vessels of the mid 19th Century that had tall masts, sharp lines, and a well-earned reputation for their extraordinary speed.

Close Aboard—This is the nautical phrase that is used to describe something that is quite near, or close alongside. (Also see Board And Board and Yardarm And Yardarm.)

Close Hauled—In sailing jargon, this nautical phrase refers to a vessel sailing as "close" (as directly into) to the wind as possible.

Close Quarters—Today this phase is typically used to mean being in close contact or in a small area, but it dates back to when vessels fought battles alongside each other with their quarters almost touching. Whenever conflicts were anticipated, temporary partitions may be installed to sub-divide officer and passenger compartments. Such "closed quarters" sometimes had small openings through which the occupants could defend themselves against enemy actions. (Also see Quarter.)

Close Reach—This nautical term refers to a vessel sailing in a wind that is coming from forward of her beam. *Trivial Tidbit*—A Close Reach is in between being *close hauled* and on a *beam reach*. (Also see Beam and Forward.)

Clove Hitch—This nautical knot consists of two half hitches, and is used to temporarily secure a line to a piling or spar. While easy to make, under tension clove hitches can be difficult to untie and may loosen after subjected to the repeated strain and release of rocking vessels. (Also see Line, Secure, and Spar.)

Coaming—This nautical term refers to a raised rim around the upper edge of a cockpit, hatch, etc. designed to keep (quite as much) water from running below. (Also see Batten Down, Cockpit, and Hatch.)

Cock Of The Walk—This phrase evolved from maritime events such as regattas or other contests held among vessels in port. The winning vessel might hoist a brightly painted wood or iron silhouette of a rooster. We currently use this phrase for a strutting, pompous individual.

Cockpit—This common term has a rather convoluted, although quite fascinating, nautical background. Since maintaining directional control is so critical during battle, warships had (and still have) a means of temporarily shifting their steering stations to safer locations below deck. In earlier times these so-called "steerage" spaces were frequently also used for tending to battle casualties, and could get as bloody as the pits in which cockfights were held. So now you know! (Also see Below Deck.)

Cofferdam—This is the nautical term for a narrow space between double bulkheads. (Also see Bulkheads.)

Coil—This is a nautical term for laying down a line or rope in the shape of circular turns. (Also see Cheese Down, Line, and Rope.)

Combing The Cat—As a subject's back started to bleed while being flogged with a cat o' nine tails, the separate flails might begin to stick to each other. Since such matted flails could result in more serious or permanent injuries, the boatswain might periodically run his fingers between them to "comb the cat" for the victim's benefit. Now there's a nice guy for you! (Also see Boatswain and Cat O' Nine Tails.)

Come About—This phrase means to bring a sailing vessel from one tack to another by turning through the eye of the wind so that the sails fly on her opposite side. (Also see Tack.)

Come Up Through The Hawse Pipe—This may or may not be a painful as it sounds, since it refers to a person who has risen from being a lowly deck hand to become a vessel's Master. (Also see Master.)

Commodore—This title is used for both: (1) the head of a yacht club, and (2) a Navy rank between Captain and Rear Admiral often held by a senior Captain with extra responsibilities. (Also see Admiral and Captain.)

Companionway—This is the nautical term used for a ladder that leads to a cabin aboard a vessel. (Also see Cabin and Ladder.)

Compass Card—This term refers to the circular card that is attached to a pivot point, and upon which are printed the thirty-two points of the compass. (Also see Boxing the Compass.)

Compass Error—This phrase is used to describe the amount that a vessel's compass reading is affected by both local magnetic variation and deviation due to the influence of nearby objects.

Corsairs—This was the term for privateers (and also pirates) who operated in the Mediterranean. The most well known were from the Barbary Coast of North Africa, and were known as "Barbary Corsairs." At least in the beginning, corsairs were authorized by one government to prey upon the vessels of another. (Also see Buccaneer, Privateer, and Pirate.)

Courtesy Flag—This refers to a small version of the national flag of the country that is being visited by a vessel. Such a flag is often flown from the visiting vessel's starboard spreader. (Also see Starboard [Side].)

Cow Hitch—While you may try using one to harness a team of cows (but why?), this phrase actually refers to an improvised knot or one that slips from being improperly tied. (Also see Rogue Knot.)

Coxswain—(pronounced *cox'n*) This was originally the title given the person responsible for a small rowboat called a "cockboat," that was one of several boats that British warships were required to carry. It has evolved into meaning a person who steers any boat and is in charge of its crew. (Also see Boat and Crew.)

Cradle—This term may be used to refer to a support for: (1) carrying a boat on a ship's deck, and (2) storing a vessel on dry land. The latter may be the safest place for some boaters. (Also see Boat and Ship.)

Cranky—These days this word is often used to describe an irritable individual, but it may have evolved from the Dutch term for a sailing vessel that was unstable due to her lack of ballast, imbalanced cargo, or faulty design. Any of these are enough to make her skipper a little bit cranky. (Also see Ballast and Skipper.)

Crew—This term originally referred to all personnel serving in a vessel, except for her Master. There was a contract between the Master and the rest of the crew. (Also see Master and Ship's Articles.) (Photograph Courtesy of the Naval Historical Center)

Crew Cut—This common term came from the days when Navy crews were given (at least monthly) haircuts *en masse* to keep their hair, beards, and moustaches neatly trimmed and so very stylish.

Crew's Mess—This name for the place where crewmembers eat originated back when crews were split into "messes" of eight to ten men each to make the distribution of food more efficient. Their cuisine often consisted of dried beans of peas, potatoes, salted meat, and bread (soft tack), which quickly became hardtack. (Also see Mess, Hardtack, and Lobscouse.)

Crossing The Line—This nautical phrase describes a rite that is highly regarded among mariners. It originally referred to the first time that a Pollywog crossed the equator aboard a ship, and was inducted into the *Order of Shellbacks* by King Neptune and other characters during a shipboard ceremony. Some spin-offs include becoming *Golden Dragons* for crossing the Date Line, *Blue Noses* for the Arctic Circle, *Frozen Stiffs* for the Antarctic Circle, and *Mossbacks* for rounding Cape Horn. (Also see Neptune, Pollywog, Shellback, and Ship.)

Crow's Nest—Crows and ravens played important roles in early coastal navigation, and sailors often transported them in cages that were secured to their vessel's mast. After lookouts began to stand watches high upon the mast in order to see longer distances, their perches became know as "Crow's Nests." (Also see As The Crow Flies, Bird's Nest, Mast, and Watches.)

Cuddy—This nautical term refers to a small cabin located in the forward part of a boat. (Also see Boat, Cabin, and Forward.)

Cup Of Joe—Josephus Daniels was appointed as the Secretary of the Navy back in 1913, and one of his least popular reforms was the abolishment of the officers' wine mess. Since then, a cup of Navy coffee became known as a "cup of Joe." Thanks a lot, Joe!

Cut And Come Again—This is the nautical term for food that was left on a vessel's mess table for the convenience of her crew. If you think about it for a while, the words may make some sense. (Also see Crew's Mess.)

Cut And Run—If one vessel's Captain sighted a larger enemy vessel, he may decide discretion was the better part of valor and order his crew to cut their anchor rode or the reef lines on their sails and run away before the wind. This phrase is still used to denote a hurried departure. (Also see Captain, Crew, Line, Reef Lines, and Rode.)

Cut His Painter—This nautical phrase can just mean that somebody has gone on their way or has deserted, or something much more serious. Since a sailor's painter is also the slang term for his lifeline, this phrase might also indicate that he has joined the great fleet in the sky. (Also see Gone Aloft.)

Cutlass—This is the term used for a curved, short sword that is often associated with nautical hand-to-hand combat, pirates, etc. (Also see Pirate.)

Cut Of His Jib—Now days this phrase is often used to mean judging somebody or something on initial appearance, but it originated when vessels of some nations might by identified by their jibs while others cut their foresails thinner so that they could maintain point and avoid being blown off course. If upon sighting an unknown vessel in the distance a Captain did not like the "cut of his jib," he might have the chance to escape and avoid a conflict. (Also see Jib.)

Cutter—This term originally referred to a relatively small, single-mast sailing vessel with a fore-and-aft rigged mainsail and two headsails. Cutters were rigged similarly to sloops, but often had a topmast and a sliding bowsprit. Due to their speed and ease of handling, revenue cutters were used to pursue smugglers. The name cutter is still used in today's Coast Guard. (Also see Bowsprit, Fore-And-Aft, Revenue Cutter, and Sloop.) (Figure Courtesy of J. Wilkinson)

D

Davits—This is the term for pieces of deck equipment with sheaves or blocks at their ends and which project over a vessel's sides to launch, retrieve, or stow small boats, etc. (Also see Boat and Deck.)

Davy Jones Locker—It is generally accepted that Davy Jones refers to a mythological devil, and ruler of the evil spirits of the sea. But some say that Davy Jones was an owner of a 16th Century London pub where unwary men were drugged and shoved into lockers, then later awaken to find themselves hijacked, shanghaied, or pressed into service on board ships. In any case, this phrase is most commonly used to mean the ocean's floor; an eternal resting place for items lost over the side, sunken vessels, and souls of those buried at sea. (Also see Hijack, Overboard, Pressed Into Service, Shanghaied, and Ship.)

Dead Horse—This phrase continues to be used today to describe advance pay. When sailors spent long periods of time ashore between voyages, they frequently ran up bills at local boarding houses. When they signed aboard a vessel, they might be advanced up to a month's pay just to clear such debts. During their first month at sea, they worked to repay such an advance. Trying to get extra work out of them during this time was often described as being akin to "flogging a dead horse." At the end of the first month at sea, a horse effigy often was ceremoniously burned to celebrate paying off their "dead horses."

Dead In The Water—A sailing vessel is dead in the water if she is becalmed with no wind in her sails, while a power vessel may be dead in the water after an engineering casualty. These days, we use this phrase to mean something or someone that is "not going anywhere." (Also see Becalm.)

Dead Rise—This rather morbid-sounding nautical term actually refers to the angle that a vessel's bottom makes relative to the horizontal.

Dead Run—This sailing term refers to a condition in which the wind comes from directly behind a vessel.

Dead Marines—This term can be traced back to William IV, who was called the "Sailor King" because he joined the Navy as a young midshipman and rose to the rank of Rear Admiral through his own merits, not through his birthright. He once asked a Steward to remove the empty "dead Marines" from the table to make room for new bottles. When a Royal Marine officer objected, the King explained that no offense was meant since, "Like Marines, these bottles had nobly sacrificed and would do so again!" *Trivial Tidbit*—Dead Marines remain upright. (Also see Steward.)

Debark—Before any Sierra Club or SPCA members get too upset, you ought to know that this is not something one does to either a tree or to a noisy canine. It means to leave a vessel, or disembark.

Deck—This refers to a vessel's nearly horizontal, i.e., slightly cambered and sloping, surfaces above her cabin and upon which people move about. Now that you know this, hit the deck! (Also see Cabin.)

Deep Six—This nautical phrase is based upon the fact that a fathom equals six feet. It originally referred to throwing an object overboard, but it has come to mean simply getting rid of something. (Also see Fathom and Overboard.)

Deliver A Broadside—Now days this phrase usually refers to an all-out verbal assault, but originally it meant simultaneously firing all of the guns on one side of a vessel. A big boom! (Also see Broadside.)

Derrick—This term refers to a system of levers used for cargo handling aboard a vessel, but the term actually came from the last name of a well-known English hangman in the 16th Century.

Dig Deep—This phrase meaning to "try harder" was originally a rowing term that meant to put one's oar deep in the water.

Dingbat—Long before Archie Bunker came along, this was a slang term for a small swab that was made from rope and was typically used for drying a vessel's decks. (Also see Deck and Rope.)

Dinghy—This is the nautical term for a small boat often carried upon, or towed behind, a larger vessel. You may recall the old song, "He's got the cutest little dinghy in the Navy." (Also see Boat.)

Dink—This nifty little term is a nickname for a dinghy. Isn't it simply precious? (Also see Dinghy.)

Displacement Hull—This is used to describe a hull design that relies on displacing an amount of water that is at least equal in weight to the vessel's weight for buoyancy. Such a vessel generally tends to be more fuel efficient, but slower, than a vessel with a planing hull. (Also see Planing Hull.)

Displacement Speed—This is the theoretical maximum speed that a vessel with a displacement hull can achieve. This is also sometimes referred to as a vessel's hull speed. (Also see Hull Speed.)

Ditty Bag—This term originally referred to a small canvas sack that was called a "ditto bag," because it typically held at least two each of things such as needles, buttons, etc. Ditty bags evolved into meaning places where sailors kept personal items, etc.

Dock—In nautical terms, this term is used for: (1) a typically man-made structure that is built to accommodate the mooring, loading/unloading, and embarking/debarking of vessels, and (2) the actual procedure of bringing a vessel alongside such a structure and securing it. (Also see Debark, Embark, Mooring, and Secure.)

Dog—This nautical term stems from the 1400s, when it was typically used for something that had a close connection with, or overlapped, something else. Now days, one of the most common uses of this term refers to a lever, that when turned overlaps a frame to lock down a hatch, etc. (Also see Hatch.)

Dog Days Of Summer—Even if they were not required for steering, watch keeping, or adjusting sails, crewmembers standing the dog watches were required to remain on deck just in case they were needed. Because they were traditionally not assigned other maintenance tasks during these times, the crew might be found on deck relaxing, playing games, spinning yarns, etc. The phrase "Dog Days Of Summer" has evolved into meaning carefree days during which only most essential tasks take place. (Also see Deck, Dog Watch, and Spinning Yarns.)

Doghouse—This was the nautical term for a small, low deckhouse used to accommodate personnel on overcrowded vessels. It probably smelled worse than a real doghouse.

Dogs Running Before Their Master—This nautical phrase actually refers to swell waves that arrive ahead of a distant storm.

Dog Watch—This nautical phrase refers to the shipboard watches that last two hours each, from 4-6 and 6-8 PM. Some sources say that the word "dog" was derived from the term "dodge," in that by breaking up the schedule in this way, one might escape having to always stand the same watch. (Also see Watches.)

Dolphins—A long time before Flipper became a television star, this was a nautical term for the (sometimes highly decorated) pilings placed in harbors to aid with the mooring of vessels.

Dolphin Striker—This was the nickname for the martingale boom on the bow of a sailing vessel. It sometimes went deep beneath the water's surface as the vessel's bow fell, and this was an area where wild dolphins liked to ride bow waves. Watch out Flipper, here it comes again! (Also see Bow.)

Donkey Boat—This was the name given to a small power boat that sailing vessels may launch to provide towing services if tugs were not available. (Also see Boat.)

Donkey Engine—As steam power became more common, these small engines began to replace sailors' muscles for heavy hauling tasks aboard more vessels. (Also see Norwegian Steam.)

Donkey's Breakfast—This colorful nautical phrase is what merchant seamen used to call their straw-stuffed bedding. On a voyage's last day, the remnants were sometimes burned or cast overboard.

Dory—Some say that the name for this small, flat-bottomed, double-ended boat with flaring sides was derived from the word "Pescadores," for Portuguese fishermen. Known for their stability and for being able to carry heavy loads, dories were sometimes carried aboard larger vessels and used for fishing in the open ocean. Many of them had removable seats, etc. so they could be more easily stacked for transporting on deck. (Also see Boat.)

Doubloons—These early Spanish coins were quite common between the 16th and the 18th Centuries. They often had an image of the King of Spain upon one side and a coat of arms upon the other. This  one was worth eight Escudos, but what can you buy for eight Escudos these days?

Down The Hatch—This familiar drinking toast originated from the lowering of cargo into a vessel's below deck hold(s). The vessel appeared to be swallowing her cargo. (Also see Below Deck, Hatch, Hold, and Toasting.)

Draft—This term is used to mean: (1) a beer, (2) a pulling horse, (3) a chilly breeze, or (4) the depth of water needed to float a vessel. It is not the depth of beer that is needed to float a pulling horse in a chilly breeze.

Dragging Your Anchor—These days we use this phrase to denote that someone is hesitant or tired. It originally referred to the last-ditch effort used by vessels that were caught in storms and headed for the rocks by lowering their anchors to drag along the bottom, desperately hoping that they would bite.

Dressed From The Dolly Shop—Dolly shops were stores where sailors could buy old clothes, etc. This phrase meant a person was poorly attired (and on Mr. Blackwell's Worst Dressed List).

Dressed To The Nines—As they approached their home waters, vessels may be "dressed" in flags and bunting. Flags might be strung from the bowsprit over the masts to the sternpost, with bunting placed along the sides. On very special occasions such as coronations, the entire ship's company dressed in their best clothes might line up on the vessel's nine primary yards in a salute to their new monarch. (Also see Bowsprit, Mast, Ship's Company, and Yard.)

Dressing Down—This phrase originally referred to the practice of treating thin and worn sails to renew their effectiveness. These days however, it means to receive a reprimand or a scolding.

Dressing Ship—When a vessel is "dressed," the national ensign is flown from her flagstaff, and usually also from each masthead. When such a vessel is "full-dressed," a rainbow of signal flags is also strung from the waterline at her bow over the mastheads to the waterline at her stern, with the end of the string traditionally weighted by a Champagne bottle. US Navy vessels are "dressed" on national holidays, and "full dressed" on the Fourth of July and Washington's Birthday from 0800 until sunset while they are not underway. (Also see Bow, Ensign, Stern, and Water-line.)

Drogue—This is an open-ended cone or a parachute-shaped device that is made out of canvas or synthetic material, and used to create drag in heavy weather. Also called a sea anchor. (Also see Sea Anchor.)

Drunk As A Fiddler—This phrase came from the custom that fiddlers who accompanied chanteys were typically paid in liquor. Play it again, Sam, if you can find your fiddle! (Also see Chantey.)

Duffle Bag—(also spelled *duffel*) This originally referred to both a sailor's sea bag and to the principal clothing items that it contained. The name came from the town of Duffel, where inexpensive but very serviceable fabric was made.

Dungarees—This name for sailors' work trousers dates back to the 1700s, when a type of sturdy Indian fabric called *dungri* was commonly used for sails. In those days sailors made their hammocks and work clothes out of this tan sailcloth so frequently that Captains in both the American and the British navies often reported that more than the actual amount of sail had been lost in battle just so their crews could make new work clothes and repair their hammocks. By that time, *dungri* had evolved into the word "dungaree," and the clothing made out of it had taken on that name. (Also see Captain, Crew, and Hammocks.)

Dunnage—This nautical term originally referred to the loose wood or other material placed on top of ballast in a vessel's hold so that cargo could be stowed upon it. These days it is nautical slang for someone's baggage or clothing, although technically it is still "packing material." (Also see Ballast and Hold.)

Dutch Courage—Today we use this phrase to denote false courage induced by alcohol, but it came from the Anglo-Dutch wars in the 17th

Century when insults and propaganda were plentiful on both sides. In this case, the British claimed that the Dutch were too cowardly to fight until they had been fortified with copious amounts of schnapps.

E

Eight Bells And All Is Well—The ship's bell was struck for each half-hour of a watch. Since most (but not all) watches were four hours in length, an announcement of, "Eight bells and all is well!" meant that such a watch had been completed and conditions aboard were normal. (Also see Ship's Bells and Watches.)

Embark—This simply means to go aboard a vessel. On your next cruise, you might want to do this at embarkation time. (Also see Debark.)

Ensign—This term is used to refer to: (1) the national flag, and (2) the most junior rank held by commissioned officers in the US Navy (that is, ever since the rank was created back in 1862.) The latter usage stems from the days when medieval knights often let their squires carry their colors (ensigns) into battle. (Photograph Courtesy of the Naval Historical Center)

Eyes Of The Ship—Many early vessels had carvings of their patrons or mythological creatures on their bows, since sailors believed that their eyes would help guide them through hazardous seas. One yarn tells of a young seaman who offered his love two precious gemstones on the day before he sailed, but she refused them. Rejected, he placed the stones in the eyes of his ship's figurehead. After changing her mind that night, his sweetheart removed the stones but did not tell him. The third day out his ship was lost with all hands in a storm because, it was said, she had stolen the ship's eyes. After his love heard the news, she cried herself to sleep. When she awoke she was blind, and the two jewels were missing forever. (Also see Bow, Figurehead, Head, Ship, and Yarn.)

F

Fairlead—This refers to a vessel's rigging hardware that is used to control, or to change, the direction taken by a line. (Also see Line.)

Fairway—This nautical term was used for the channel of a river, narrow bay, etc., long before any golf courses. So cast off, but be sure to yell, "Fore!" as you get underway. (Also see Cast Off and Underway.)

Fair Winds And Following Seas—This is a common nautical expression among sailors for "Best Wishes!"

Fake—This nautical term refers to arranging or coiling a line in an ornamental fashion so that each loop lies in a figure eight or a circular pattern that is almost flat on the deck. (Also see Coil, Deck, and Line.)

Fantail—This nautical tem refers to the afterdeck overhang at the stern of a vessel. (Also see Stern.)

Fast—Not so fast, matey! This term actually means that one object is secured to another, e.g., "Make that line fast to a cleat!" (Also see Cleat, Line, and Secure.)

Fathom—This was originally a land measuring term derived from the Anglo-Saxon word *faethm*, and was actually once defined by an act of Parliament as, "the length of a man's arms around the object of his affections." A fathom equals six feet, but we also use the term to mean that one is trying to "embrace" a concept or figure out something.

Feathering Oars—This refers to turning an oar's blade into a horizontal position when the oar is being taken back for the next stroke. This may reduce its drag, and conserve energy.

Feeling Blue—The nautical origin of this expression may surprise you. Whenever a vessel lost her Master or officers on her voyage, the crew might fly a blue flag and paint a blue band along the sides of her hull while she was returning home. (Also see Crew, Master, and Officer.) (Figure Courtesy of the US Navy)

Fender—This is the nautical term for cushions temporarily hung over the side to protect a vessel from chafing when she is lying alongside a dock, or another vessel. Landlubbers sometimes call these "bumpers." (Also see Dock and Landlubber.)

Fend Off—This is an extremely handy, i.e., essential, skill for all new boaters. It means to prevent one vessel from striking another vessel, dock, piling, pier, auto, aircraft, building, etc. (Also see Dock and Pier.)

Fid—This rather odd nautical term is the name for a pointed tool used to separate the strands of a rope or line. (Also see Line, Marlinspike, and Rope.)

Fiddler's Green—In this imaginary paradise "mates were not allowed and pockets never emptied," and weary mariners could partake in wine, women, and song free from the daily hardships of their seafaring lives. Fiddlers would gather around 17th Century village greens, and provide ambiance for sailors' pleasures, e.g., chess, backgammon, offered by the surrounding establishments.

Fiddles—The nautical use of this term refers to fittings that were clamped onto a vessel's dining tables during heavy weather to limit the movement of plates, glasses, landlubbers, etc.

Figure Eight Knot—This nautical knot is often used to prevent a line from passing through a rigging block or a grommet. (Also see Line.)

Figurehead—These days we use this term to describe a person whose main function is to inspire confidence within an organization. Carved ornamental figures on sailing vessels' bows were initially religious or protective symbols, but later were for purely decorative purposes. (Also see Bow, Eyes Of The Ship, and Head.)

Filibuster—Although today this is a political term meaning to delay or to obstruct the passage of legislation by non-stop speechmaking, it was also what buccaneers and smugglers were once called in England. The French word *flibustier* came from the Dutch term for freebooter, as in "free booty." (Also see Booty and Buccaneer.)

Finger Pier—This refers to a narrow pier which projects from shore, or is perpendicular to a larger pier. (Also see Dock and Pier.)

First Navy Jack—As of 11 September 2002, all US Navy vessels were ordered to again fly the First Navy Jack instead of the familiar Union Jack during the war on terrorism. The former consists of a picture of a rattlesnake superimposed upon a field of red and white stripes and above the motto, "Don't Tread On Me." It was also the signal used by Commodore Hopkins to engage the British during the US War of Independence. (Also see Union Jack.) (Figure Courtesy of the US Navy)

First Navy Jack

First Rate—Now days this phrase is often used to imply a degree of excellence, but it goes back to when Royal Navy ships were rated by how many heavy cannon they had. A line-of-battle ship with 100 or more guns was designated a First Rate, while Second through Sixth Rates each had fewer heavy cannons. Now go count your cannons to see how you rate! (Also see Ship.)

Fits The Bill—Today this phrase is used to mean something that meets current needs, but it originally referred to the "Bills of Lading" signed by vessels' Masters as receipts for loaded goods and promises to deliver them to their destination in the same condition. If everything was in order when these delivered goods were checked, they were said to "fit the bill." (Also see Master.)

Flake Out—To keep a vessel's anchor chain in good condition, it would be periodically laid out fore-and-aft (flaked) on her deck so any worn or weak links could be located and replaced. As a precaution against fouling, the Captain/Master may also order the crew to "flake out" the anchor chain on deck when preparing to anchor the vessel. Sometimes we need to "flake out" in the sunshine, like those anchor chains. (Also see Captain, Deck, Fore-And-Aft, and Master.)

Flemish Down—This refers to laying down the unused portion of a line or a rope in an ornamental fashion that resembles figure eights, so it is ready to run out without kinking. (Also see Fake, Line, and Rope.)

Flogging the Monkey—This old expression refers to getting a weak drink by rinsing out an empty rum barrel (called a monkey) with water. Today it is mostly done at spring breaks. (Also see Binge and Monkey.)

Floor—Yes Virginia, ships can also have floors. They are the nearly horizontal platforms on the very bottom of a vessel, on each side of her keelson. (Also see Keelson.)

Floozies—Although we know there is no modern analogy, but once upon a time this term was applied to loose women who frequented waterfront taverns and were even sometimes allowed on board during long periods in port. Maybe those really were the good ole days!

Flotsam—This is a legal term in maritime law that refers to floating items accidentally lost over the side, or left from a wrecked or lost ship. (Also see Jetsam and Lagan.)

Flunky—Today we use this term interchangeably with lackey, minion, brown nose, toady, suck-up, etc.; but it was once the nickname for an Officers' Steward or a Wardroom Attendant. (Also see Officer, Steward, and Wardroom.)

Fly-By-Night—Today we use this phrase to describe a questionable operation, but it was originally the term for a large sail used for sailing downwind that required relatively little attention. These characteristics made it quite useful for sailing during darkness by individuals who dealt in contraband, and who came to be known as "fly-by-nighters."

Flying Dutchman—Legend says that any mariner who sees the Flying Dutchman ghost ship will die within the day. After failing to round both the Cape of Good Hope as well as Cape Horn, the cursed ship continued on her endless voyage with her white-haired crew crying out for help. An actual Flying Dutchman set sail in 1660…so is she real or just a legend?

Following Sea—This is the nautical term used to describe waves approaching from astern, and moving in the same general direction as the vessel. (Also see Astern, Fair Winds And Following Seas, and Pooped.)

Footloose—The phrase "footloose and fancy free" is used today for somebody who lacks commitment, but the word originally referred to the bottom of a sail called its foot. If it was not properly secured to the boom the sail was said to be "footloose," and flogged in the wind with a mind of its own.

Fore-and-Aft—This nautical phrase is used to denote a lengthwise orientation with a vessel, as opposed to being oriented (more or less) perpendicular to her keel. (Also see Athwartships.)

Fore-And-Aft Rigged—This phrase refers to sails that lie in a (more or less) lengthwise direction of a vessel, as opposed to being oriented (more or less) perpendicular to her keel as on a square-rigger. (Also see Keel and Square-Rigger.)

Forecastle—(pronounced fok'sul) This nautical term refers to the forward part of the main deck, and came from days when wooden "castles" were built upon the forward and after sections of the deck from which archers shot arrows and others threw spears, etc. during battle. This term is also used to describe the forward compartment in which sailors were berthed. (Also see Berth, Deck, Forward, and Main Deck.)

Forefoot—This term refers to the point where a vessel's stem joins the forward end of her keel. (Also see Forward, Keel, Stem, Under Foot.)

Foremast—On vessels with two or more masts and a larger mast abaft, this term refers to the mast nearest the bow. (Also see Abaft, Bow, and Mast.)

Forward—This nautical term is used to mean toward, near, or at, a vessel's bow. The opposite of forward is the term aft. (Also see Aft and Bow.)

Foul Up—Today this phrase is commonly used to describe a person who messes things up on a rather regular basis. The word "foul" in this case evolved out of the nautical term that means something is impeded or entangled, e.g., a foul anchor is one that is entangled in line or cable. (Also see Line.)

Founder—This nautical term refers to when a vessel fills with water and sinks. This is usually not a very good thing to do!

Freeboard—This term refers to the minimum vertical distance from the surface of the water to the vessel's gunwale. It can be very important if you like staying dry. (Also see Bulwark and Gunwale.)

From Stem-To-Stern—Now days we use this phrase to mean doing a thorough job, but it was derived from the fact that the very forward end of a vessel is called her stem, while the rear is called her stern. Therefore, doing something from stem-to-stern means that it encompasses the entire vessel. (Also see Forward, Stem, and Stern.)

Fudge—Most do not realize that using this term to mean, "bending the truth" is said to have come from Captain Fudge in the 17th Century, who was nicknamed, "Lying Fudge" because he was such a notorious fabricator of untruths.

Furl—This term means to fold or to roll up a sail up snugly, and to secure it to its main support, e.g., a yard. (Also see Secure, Unfurl, and Yard.)

G

Galleon—This is the term for a moderate to large sized sailing vessel that evolved from the Carrack, but did not have as high a forecastle. Galleons had three or more masts, were square-rigged on their fore and Main Masts, and lateen-rigged on their after masts. They were popular warships for both England and Spain during the 1500s, but were also used as merchant trading vessels. Galleons were narrower and longer than Carracks, and also more maneuverable. (Also see Carrack, Forecastle, Foremast, Lateen, Main Mast, and Mast.) (Figure Courtesy of J. Wilkinson)

Galleon

Galley—This nautical term has two principal meanings. The first refers to a type of Mediterranean fighting vessel that dates back to about 3000 B.C. The earliest versions were propelled solely by oars manned by slaves, but some later ones (like the Galley that used by the infamous Captain Kidd) also carried sails. One principal weapon was a beakhead on their bow, designed to ram enemy vessels. Because the rowing tiers made it hard to mount guns on their sides, the Galleys had to mount them on their beakheads. This meant that they could only fire in a generally forward direction. Although Galleys were fast and were not totally dependent on the wind, they could not carry very heavy armament and were at risk in heavy weather. Some insist that the second use of this term for a vessel's kitchen originated with the early use of Galley slaves as cooks, but others maintain it came from the brick or stone "gallery" amidships where early sailors cooked meals. (Also see Amidships, Beakhead, Bow, Forward, and Head.)

Galley Pepper—This was the term for soot or ashes that often fell into food being prepared in a vessel's galley. Season your burgoo with a pinch of chimney soot, and…Bam! (Also see Burgoo, Galley, and Lobscouse.)

Gam—This began as a slang term for a pod of whales, but evolved into meaning an at-sea conference between whaling ship Masters. One usually began with the two vessels sailing close enough so their Masters could speak more easily. Then one of the Masters, his officers, and any shipboard wives might be rowed over to the other vessel to exchange news, mail, and scuttlebutt. Today, this term means a nautical bull session. (Also see Master, Officer, and Scuttlebutt.)

Gang Plank—This is the nautical term used for the temporary walkway placed between a vessel and a dock, pier, etc., and it is also the basis for the phrase, "walk the plank." (Also see Dock, Gangway, and Pier.)

Gangway—This nautical term is used for: (1) a narrow, often portable platform used by persons boarding or leaving a vessel moored alongside a pier, (2) that part of the vessel's side amidships where people can pass in and out, and (3) an command meaning to, "Clear the way!" (Also see Amidships, Moor, and Pier.)

Garbled—These days, a distorted or mixed up message is said to be "garbled." In earlier times, *garbling* referred to the illegal practice of mixing rubbish in with the vessel's cargo.

Garboard—Believe it or not, this nautical term is not related to either starboard or larboard. It refers to the first plank (on a wooden vessel) or plate (on a steel vessel) of the outer hull that is adjacent to her keel. But you already knew that, right? (Also see Keel, Larboard, Planking, and Starboard {Side].)

Gee dunk—This is a nautical term that is sometimes used for snacks, candy, ice cream, etc. (Also see Lollywater.)

Get Knotted—This old nautical term just means, "Get Lost!"

Give Way!—This command was given to men in a boat to start rowing, or to pull with full force. (Also see Boat.)

Give-Way Vessel—This is another term that is sometimes used to describe the vessel that should yield in overtaking, meeting, or crossing situations. (Also see Burdened Vessel and Rules Of The Road.)

Giving A Wide Berth—Now days we use this phase to suggest keeping away from something or someone dangerous or in a bad mood, but it originally referred to mooring far enough from other vessels or objects to avoid collisions when swinging on the tide or the wind.

Giving Leeway—Wise mariners keep well off a dangerous lee (downwind) shore, just in case they need extra maneuvering room in an emergency. These days, we use this phrase to mean being more patient or tolerant of somebody. (Also see Lee, Lee Shore, Mariner, and Sea Room.)

Glimmer—This colloquialism came from the nautical term "glim" for a lantern, lamp, candle, or any other type of light source.

Going Down The Mine—This phrase refers to a boat that is speeding down the face of a wave with no apparent escape route. (Also see Boat.)

Going Great Guns—Today we hear this phrase in reference to something that is a roaring success, but it originated from the Navy use of the term "great guns" for large caliber (mounted) weapons.

Going Off On Another Tack—Today this phrase is used to mean taking a different course of action. It comes from the sailing term tack, which describes a vessel progressing in a zigzag fashion by moving obliquely into the wind. Now isn't that clear? (Also see Tack.)

Gone Aloft—This is another term for a sailor who had died. (Also see Cut His Painter.)

Gone By The Board—Today this phase is often used to denote something that is no longer relevant or someone who is passé, but it dates back to the days when the sides of ships were referred to as "boards." It was used to describe anything seen to have gone overboard or seen floating past the vessel's side. It was also used to mean disposing of objects that are of no further use over the side. (Also see Board, By The Boards, and Overboard.)

Gripe—These days we use this term to describe complaining about something. But sailing vessels are said to gripe if they tend to end up with their bows into the wind when they sail close to the wind, either because of sail imbalance or poor design. When this occurs their sails flog around, they are hard to control, and little or no forward progress is made. (Also see Bow.)

Grog—Back In 1740, British Admiral Vernon was called "Old Grog" for the cloaks made out of a cloth called grogram that he wore until they were extremely threadbare. After he had his crew's daily rum rations diluted, the watered-down result became known as "grog," because it was said to be as thin as his cloaks. In the adjacent photograph, British sailors during the early 1900s are dipping their daily grog from a cask that is labeled "God Bless." *Trivial Tidbit*—Cap-
tain Bucko's recipe for grog calls for: two ounces of rum, two teaspoons of sugar, six ounces of water, and a dash of limejuice (to prevent scurvy).

Enjoy, but don't get too groggy! (Also see Crew.) (Photograph Courtesy of the Naval Historical Center)

Ground Swell—We use this to describe a growing change in public opinion, but it originally referred to the sudden rise in water level due to arrival of swell waves from a distant storm.

Ground Tackle—This is the nautical term that is used to collectively refer to an anchor and its associated gear. (Also see Rode.)

Gunk Holing—This term refers to cruising in shallow water and staying overnight in small coves. It might not have a very fascinating nautical origin, but it is nevertheless fun to say!

Gun Salutes—When a visiting vessel fired a gun salute upon nearing a port in the early days, it was more than merely a formal gesture of her friendly intentions. Because it took so long to reload, it also indicated to those ashore that her cannons were discharged. Gun salutes were rendered in odd numbers, except if the vessel's Captain or Master had died during her voyage. Shore batteries usually had access to more powder than was available aboard ships, so salutes were not always exchanged on a shot-for-shot basis. To prevent gun salutes from becoming too costly, the British Admiralty established a rule that for every volley fired by a ship, a shore battery could return up to three shots. These same regulations also stated that the maximum number of shots a vessel could fire in one salute was seven, thus setting the maximum number returned at 7 X 3, or twenty-one. (Also see Captain, Master, Ship, and Twenty-One Gun Salute.)

Gunwale—(pronounced *gun-nel*.) This nautical term refers to the uppermost edge of a vessel's side. Most, except for sail-boaters and submariners, like to keep it above the water, but that's up to you. (Also see Bilge Pump, Founder, and Waterline.)

H

Hail From—These days this phrase is typically used to refer to a person's hometown, but it evolved from the fact that sailing vessels often hailed each other when passing. After a vessel announced her homeport, she was said to "hail from" there.

Halcyon Days—This phrase is sometimes used to describe a peaceful and tranquil time, but its origin lies in Greek mythology. Halcyone was the daughter of Aeolus, and the wife of Ceyx. After Ceyx drowned, she threw herself into the sea in grief. The gods took pity upon the lovers however, and changed them into Kingfishers, or Halcyons. Good old Zeus also forbade the wind to blow during the Halcyon's breeding season, which is just before and after the winter solstice.

Half Hitch—This is the basis for the structure of many nautical knots, it consists of one turn of a line about an object with the end led back through the line's bight (Also see Bight and Line.)

Halyards—This nautical term refers to the lines used to haul up a vessel's sails, as well as the yards, booms, etc. that hold her sails in place. It comes from the phrase, "haul yard." (Also see Line and Yard.)

Hammocks—Some say that Christopher Columbus was one of the first to adopt these swinging beds, after seeing them being used by the West Indies natives and recognizing advantages for crewmen on board rolling vessels. Early hammocks were made out of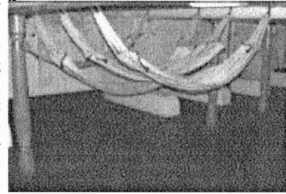

old sailcloth and were also used for burials at sea. Chris was one frugal fellow! (Photograph Courtesy of the US Navy)

Hampered Vessel—This nautical term refers to a vessel that is restricted in her maneuvering ability due to the nature of her work, e.g., towing another vessel, diving operations.

Hand Over Fist—Today this phrase means to proceed or to accumulate something quickly, but it came from the British term "hand over hand" used to describe rapidly climbing the rigging or hauling on a line. That evolved into the phrase "hand over fist" by American sailors, but it still referred to skills that were a matter of pride among mariners. (Also see Line and Mariner.)

Hand Salutes—Although the hand salute did not have a nautical origin, there are some interesting distinctions about it. While ashore hand salutes are always to be given with the right hand, sailors whose right hand or arm is encumbered may salute with their left hand. *Trivial Tidbit*—The nautical slang for a hand salute is, "throwing a fish." Think about it.

Handsomely!—This old nautical command means to do something carefully and slowly…you handsome devil!

Hang From The Yards—Being a real creative bunch, sailors dreamed up various ways to dangle a person from a vessel's yards as punishment…by their neck, but also sometimes by their toes. (Also see Yard.)

Hangman's Knots—Many folks do not realize that there were actually two knots in the line that was used to hang someone aboard a vessel. The first one was the usual hangman's noose, while the second was designed to release several feet of slack line after the victim was hoisted up to the vessel's yard/yardarm by other crewmen, resulting in a sudden drop and a snapped neck. (Also see Line, Yard, and Yardarm.)

Hard Aground—This is the nautical term used to describe a vessel that has gone aground and is incapable of re-floating herself. (Also see Aground.) (Photograph Courtesy of Captain S. Theberge and the NOAA Photo Library)

Hard Alee!—This is a warning given to those aboard that the wheel or the tiller of a sailing vessel is being turned quickly to leeward. For folks aboard small sailboats it also means, "Duck!" (Also see Aboard, Come About, Leeward, and Sailboat.)

Hard And Fast—This phrase refers to a vessel that is hard (firmly) aground, and fast (solidly) in place. If going aground is not good, why are there so many phrases for doing it? (Also see Hard Aground.)

Hard Over—This phrase refers to turning a vessel's steering mechanism as far as possible in one direction. This might not always be that wise, because jams can (and do) sometimes result.

Hardtack—This was what sailors called a ship's biscuit, which was a dietary stable for many of them. The name makes it clear this was a delightfully light and flaky puff pastry treat. Right!

Hard Up—We may use this term to mean being financially desperate, but it originally referred to when a vessel's rigging tackle blocks were as close together as possible. (Also see Chock-A-Block and Tackle.)

Hard Water Captain—This phrase is used to refer to a Captain/Master who is fearless when his vessel is sailing in harm's way. (Also see Captain and Master.)

Hasn't Got A Clue—Now days this phrase is often used to imply that someone is brainless or does not understand a situation, but some say it came from the word "clew," which refers to the corner of the sail where a ring is sown into the fabric. If it comes loose, it is said that the vessel, "Hasn't got a clew."

Hatch—This refers to an opening (and some say also to the covering for such an opening) in a vessel's deck that allows for: passage below/topside, loading/unloading cargo, etc. (Also see Below Deck and Deck.)

Hawse Pipe—This is the nautical term for a heavy-duty iron pipe that provides an opening through a vessel's hull at her bow (and sometimes also at her stern) for her anchor chain(s). (Also see Bow and Stern.)

Hawser—This is a generic term for heavy-duty rope or cable that is often used for towing or securing large vessels, etc. (Also see Rope and Secure.)

Hazing—Groups might use this to assert their authority over newcomers, but it is far from being a new practice. In the 19th Century, some Captains/Masters would work their crews for long hours to deprive them of sleep and make them generally miserable. It was called *hazing*, even back then! (Also see Captain, Crew, and Master.)

Head—There are several principal meanings of this term. The first refers to the carvings upon a vessel's prow, which may be a: ram (beakhead), figure (figurehead), or scroll-like design similar to the head of a violin (fiddlehead). The second pertains to the use of this term for a vessel's toilet, which actually relates back to the first meaning. Early vessels had no sanitary facilities, so people relieved themselves balanced upon the gunwales. Beakheads sometimes included small platforms on either side from which archers could shoot. These were designed as wooden grates to keep the weight down and also to lessen the chance they might be carried away by the passing waves. They also offered a serendipitous (what a great word), improvement to those vessels' sanitary facilities. Because these early toilets were located near the vessel's head, they took on that name. *Several Trivial Tidbits*—Passengers and officers could use "privacy heads," that were basically oak buckets or porcelain chamber pots. Sailors were told to use the leeward head (for reasons that should be obvious), but back then leeward was spelled "lewward," and pronounced "loo'ard." Could this be an origin of the term "loo?" (Also see Beakhead, Carried Away, Figurehead, Gunwales, Leeward, and Prow.)

Heading—This term is used to denote the direction in which a vessel's head (bow) is pointed at any given moment. (Also see Bow and Head.)

Heave—This term is used to mean: (1) to pull upon a line, (2) to throw a line, (3) the rising and falling of a vessel with the seas, and (4) what seasick folks do…but wait, there's more! (Also see Line.)

Heave Away—This phrase means to cast something away, e.g., "Heave away that hawser!" (Also see Hawser and Heave.)

Heave Handsomely—While it might seem a little strange, this variant means to heave gently. (Also see Handsomely and Heave.)

Heave Hearty—This variation means to heave quickly or forcefully. (Also see Heave.)

Heave In—This variant refers to hauling (pulling) something in, e.g., a line. (Also see Line.)

Heave Out—This variation actually means to get out of one's bunk, e.g., "Heave out and trice up!" (Also see Heave.)

Heave To—This nautical phrase refers to bringing a vessel into a position in which she can more safely and easily ride out heavy weather, by attempting to minimize the forces on her. Power may be reduced, her sails may be reefed, and her bow brought into the weather or seas. (Also see Bow, Heave, and Reefing.)

Heaving Line—This is the term used for a light line with a weight or a monkey fist on one end that is heaved from one vessel to another or to/ from shore, then used for hauling a heavier hawser or cable aboard/ ashore. (Also see Aboard, Hawser, Heave, Line, Messenger, and Monkey Fist.)

"Avast…that's quite enough heaving for now!"

Heel—This nautical term may be used to mean: (1) a vessel tilting over sideways due to the wind or an imbalanced load, (2) the bottom of a mast, and (3) the aft end of the keel. (Also see Aft, Keel, and Mast.)

High And Dry—This phrase often refers to somebody who is left without support or resources, but it was originally used for a vessel left "high" upon the shore and "dry" by an ebbing tide.

Highliner—This nautical term can be used to mean: (1) an individual who takes the (exciting) journey between vessels at sea via a highline, and (2) an excellent fisherman. The latter usage originated from when the best fisherman aboard got the highest spot on the deck, so that his line was above all others'. (Also see Aboard, Deck, and Line.)

High, Wide, And Handsome—Today this phrase is used to describe somebody who is in a fortunate condition, but it was originally spoken as a complement to a tall ship that rode dry and easily with a favorable wind. (Also see Tall Ship.)

Hijack—Instead of saying "Hello, Sailor!" in earlier times women of easy virtue would sometimes greet men with "Hi, Jack!" But their words lost some charm after the men were knocked out and dragged off to vessels that needed crewmen for long or arduous voyages. (Also see Shanghaied.)

Hit The Deck!—The meaning of this phrase has not changed much, except it was originally used to awaken sailors when the time had come for them to come up on deck and go to work.

Hodgepodge—Today we often use this term to describe a jumble, but it evolved from the word "hotchpotch" that was a method used to divide damaged cargo and property equally after two vessels collided and were both deemed to be responsible.

Hoisted By One's Petard—"Gotcha!" is probably a good translation of this phrase. Some maintain that it evolved from the nautical use of the term "petard" for a small keg of black powder once used to prime cannon fuses. Apparently these *petards* were kept alongside the cannons during battles for convenience sake, although wayward sparks occasionally would set one off and "hoist" the gunner into the air.

Hold—This is the nautical term for the interior space of a vessel within which her cargo is stowed.

Holy Mackerel—This rather odd exclamatory phrase has its origin in the fact that because mackerel spoils quickly, it could be sold on Sundays despite 17th Century blue laws…. thus making it holy!

Holystone—Wooden ship decks were scrubbed with pieces of sandstone called holystones, since using them brought a sailor to his knees. Large holystones were known as "Bibles," while smaller blocks known as "Prayer Books" were used to reach awkward places. (Also see Deck and Ship.)

Horse Latitudes—There are several theories about the origin of this name for these regions of light and variable winds on both sides of the equator. Some say that it came from when vessels carrying horses were becalmed for so long they were forced to throw the animals into the sea to conserve water. Others insist that the name was derived from the *Gulf of the Mares* off Spain, which exhibits similar wind conditions. Some say it came from the fact that it took early sailing vessels so long to transit through these regions their crews had sufficient time to work off their "dead horses." (Also see Becalm and Dead Horse.)

Hot Pursuit—This modern phrase stems from an unofficial principle of naval warfare that allowed fleeing vessels to be pursued into neutral waters and captured there if the chase first began in international waters. Contrary to popular belief, this was not a tactic invented by Dirty Harry!

Hulk—We sometimes use this term to refer to a person who is rather large, but with few other useful attributes. It was originally applied to old sailing vessels that were not worth making seaworthy again. Such vessels were often stripped of their rigging and used as prisons or as storage facilities.

Hull Speed—This is the theoretical maximum speed that a vessel with a displacement hull can attain, although relatively small increases may be possible with the addition of more power. Hull speed is directly proportional to waterline length, which is a reason why faster displacement hull vessels, e.g., warships, tend to be relatively long. So size does matter! (Also see Displacement Hull, Displacement Speed, and Waterline.)

Hunky-Dory—Some say that this term came from a Japanese street called *honcho-dori,* which once ran from the center of town to the waterfront. Since the establishments on that street catered to sailors' pleasures, e.g., checkers, this phrase is still used to mean an enjoyable situation!

Hydrofoil—This relatively new term refers to a vessel equipped with underwater foils (similar to wings) that use hydrodynamic force to lift her hull and reduce friction at higher forward speeds.

Hydroplane—This term is used for a type of powerboat that is designed to use hydrodynamic and sometimes also aerodynamic forces to lift its hull and skim over the water's surface at high speeds.

I

Idlers—This was the name given crewmembers that worked during days, and were excused (idle) from standing watches during the night. Many have specific nicknames, like: *Chips* for a ship's carpenter, *Boats* for a boatswain, *Blackie* for a blacksmith, *Coop* for a cooper (who made casks), *Sails* for a sail-maker, *The Doctor* for the ship's cook, and *Soups* for a cook's assistant. There are others, but that's enough now. (Also see Boatswain.)

Inboard—This term is used for: (1) a location inside or toward the center of a vessel's hull, and (2) an engine that is mounted inside a vessel with a propeller shaft that penetrates her hull.

In Irons—This refers to the condition in which: (1) a square-rigged sailing vessel is taken aback and stopped dead in the water, and (2) the bow of sailing vessel comes around to face the wind in such a way that neither side of her sails fills. (Also see Bow, Dead In The Water, and Taken Aback.)

Inland Rules—This phrase refers to that set of navigational Rules Of The Road that apply to vessels operating in lakes, rivers, inland waterways, harbors, bayous, puddles, etc. (Also see Rules Of The Road.)

In The Doldrums—We currently use this phrase to indicate somebody is depressed or in low spirits. The doldrums are areas located on both sides of the equator in lower latitudes, where very light winds and an unrelenting sun make it rather depressing for sailors. In these areas sailing vessels could be becalmed for many days, leading to demoralized crews who became even more so when ordered into rowboats to tow their ships into more favorable wind conditions. (Also see Becalm.)

In The Offing—Today this phrase is used to mean something is about to occur, but back in the 16th Century it was used to describe objects that were some distance away and barely visible, e.g., "We saw a vessel in the offing." The term "offing" referred to the sea offshore and toward the horizon.

Iron Spinnaker—This is what blow-boaters not so affectionately call an auxiliary engine in a sailing vessel. (Also see Blow-boater.)

J

Jack Nastyface—This is the nickname that is sometimes given to an unpopular crewmember.

Jack Staff—This refers to a short pole at a vessel's bow upon which the Jack (that's the flag, not the aforementioned crewmember) gets hoisted. (Also see Bow, First Navy Jack, and Union Jack.)

Jack Tar—This slang term for a sailor has been around since 1780. In early days, sailors called each other "Jack," much like some people these days use "Buddy" or even "Dude." These early sailors also often wore clothing and broad-brimmed hats made out of tar-impregnated fabric. The hats as well as the sailors who wore them became known as tarpaulins, a term that was later shortened into "tars." Others insist this term came from the fact some sailors applied tar they used on their vessel's rigging and seams to their hair. Since getting a stain on one's jumper aboard a Navy vessel could mean extra duty, sailors began wearing a removable bib on the back of their collars. Over time this became a distinct feature of sailor's uniforms. (Also see Tarpaulin.)

Jacobs Ladder—This originally referred to the web of rigging leading to a vessel's skysail, but it is more commonly used for a type of flexible ladder often lowered over the side to the waterline to let pilots embark or debark. (Also see Debark, Embark, Ladder, Pilot, and Waterline.)

Jaunty—This was the nickname given a vessel's master-at-arms, who was responsible for enforcing shipboard discipline and also for supervising disciplinary actions such as flogging. This term is a corruption of the French word *gendarme*, but some insist that the current meaning came from the fact that these folks tended to strut a bit while they flaunted their power. (Also see Master-At-Arms.)

Jetsam—This is a legal term in maritime law, referring to any goods or equipment deliberately cast over the side (jettisoned) to lighten a vessel or to make her more stable in high winds or heavy seas. (Also see Flotsam and Lagan.)

Jetty—This term refers to a man-made structure projecting from the shore, e.g., a breakwater.

Jib—This is the nautical term used for a triangularly shaped foresail that is forward of a vessel's foremast. (Also see Cut Of His Jib, Foremast, and Forward.)

Jibber The Kibber—This phrase refers to "wreckers" decoying vessels onto the rocks by displaying false lights. (Also see Mooncusser.)

Jolly Roger—Many pirates created their own flags that they thought would strike fear in their victims. Pirates in the West Indies once flew (blood) red flags so people would know who they were. Most think of the infamous Skull And Cross Bones, but it was only one variation.

There were many other designs, such as the flag shown here flown by the pirate Bartholomew Roberts, who was nicknamed "Le Jolie Rogue." Some say that the term Jolly Roger was a corruption of *Jolie Rougere*, a red flag once flown by French buccaneers to indicate that no quarter would be given. In certain parts of the Caribbean the Jolly Roger meant the pirates were willing to take prisoners, whereas a red pennant signified that a vessel's crew and passengers would be slaughtered. (Also see Blackjack, Pirate, No Quarter, and Skull And Cross Bones.)

Junk—This term may refer to: (1) the stuff we all have in our garages; (2) old condemned rope; and (3) a flat-bottomed, squared-bowed, high-sterned, sailing vessel from the Far East. (Also see Rope.)

Jury Rig—We sometimes use this phrase for things that are hurriedly slapped together to make do, but it evolved out of the term "jury mast," referring to a temporary mast that was made from any available spar when a vessel's original mast was broken or lost at sea. (Also see Mast and Spar.)

K

Kedge—This term is used for: (1) moving by setting out an anchor then pulling the vessel toward it by hauling on the anchor rode, and (2) a type of small auxiliary anchor. (Also see Rode.)

Keel—This refers to the lowermost and principal structural member of a vessel that runs fore-and-aft along the entire length of her centerline from stem to stern, and supports her frame. The keel also serves two other functions in modern sailboats: (1) it allows one to sail closer into the wind, and (2) its weight makes a vessel with a keel less likely to capsize than a sailboat with a centerboard. (Also see Centerline, Centerboard, Fore-And-Aft, Sailboat, Stem, and Stern.)

Keelhauling—This form of punishment for serious offenses is said to have originated with the Dutch, but it was adopted by other navies during the 15th and 16th Centuries. Offenders were dropped into the sea then hauled beneath the vessel. Cannons were sometimes also fired to warn others not to risk this usually fatal process. The United States Navy did not endorse keelhauling.

Keel Over—Today this expression is often used to describe the results of a severe emotional or physical blow, but it also refers to the situation when a strong gust of wind causes a vessel to capsize with her keel pointed upward. This is not very good in either case! (Also see Keel.)

Keelson—This is the nautical term for a vessel's internal keel that is laid in the center of her floor timbers over the top of, and parallel to, her principal keel. (Also see Floor and Keel.)

Keep A Sharp Lookout—Today this is a caution to be alert, but it originated from the posting of lookouts aloft or on the bow of a vessel to keep watch for potential dangers. (Also see Bow.)

Keeping On An Even Keel—These days this phrase might be offered as advice to keep one's emotions in check, but it once referred to trimming the sails so that an equal amount of water passed by both sides of the vessel.

Ketch—This is the nautical term used for a two-mast sailboat with a mizzenmast that is shorter than and abaft her main mast, but is located forward of her helm. *Trivial Tidbit*—If such a vessel's helm is forward of her mizzenmast however, she is called a yawl. (Also see Abaft, Forward, Main Mast, Mizzenmast, Sailboat, and Yawl.) (Figure Courtesy of J. Wilkinson)

Ketch

Khaki—This material did not become a naval uniform option until the 20th Century, but it has an interesting background. While serving in India during the mid-1800s British soldiers often soaked their white uniforms in coffee, mud, curry powder, etc. so they would be less visible (targets) in the field. From this one must assume that it was better to be smelled, than to be seen, in those days.

Knocked Down—This phrase refers to a vessel that has been rolled on her beam ends or completely over by a gust of wind, etc. If properly ballasted, she should right herself quickly. (Also see Ballast and Beam Ends.)

Knock Off!—This was an actual order to cease work on board a vessel. The basic meaning has not changed that much.

Knot—This unit of speed equates to one nautical mile (which is about 6076 feet) an hour. It was coined when a line having knots evenly spaced at specific intervals and a log chip attached to one end was used to measure a vessel's speed. The chip on the end of this "log line" was thrown over the stern, where it remained (more or less) in one place. The line was allowed to run free for a specific time period then hauled back aboard. The knots that had passed over the stern during that time were counted to measure her speed. Today however, most people prefer to use the Global Positioning System, etc. (Also see Aboard, Line, Nautical Mile, and Stern.)

Knows The Ropes—There were miles of lines on larger sailing vessels, and they were not color-coded. In the early days, if this phrase was written upon a seaman's papers it indicated that he was still a novice, i.e., all he knew about seamanship was the names and uses of the principal lines. But over time it came to mean almost the exact opposite, and today we use this phrase to describe a knowledgeable individual. (Also see Line.)

Kraken—This was the name given to an enormous sea monster reportedly seen off of the coasts of North America and Norway. Kraken was so large that it was sometimes mistaken for an island. Now that's big!

L

Labor—This nautical term is used to describe when a vessel pitches, rolls, or otherwise struggles while underway in heavy seas. In this case, deep breathing might not help that much.

Ladder—This is the correct nautical term for both vertical and inclined "steps" on board a vessel. These include: boarding ladders, companionways, swim ladders, etc. Do not say staircase!

Lagan—This complements the more familiar terms of flotsam and jetsam, and refers to objects that are cast over the side with lines or buoys attached so they can be retrieved later. (Also see Flotsam, Jetsam, and Line.)

Land Breeze—This term refers to a wind that blows from the land toward the water, often when the air temperature over the land cools below the air temperature over the water.

Landfall—This nautical term refers to arriving ashore after being at sea. Making a good landfall means coming ashore where and when one intended, which is usually preferred!

Land Ho!—This is the cry shouted when land is first sighted. It is rarely used when operating in ponds or small streams.

Landing In Debt—Debt was around well before credit cards, and this phrase originally referred to a mariner who arrived ashore owing debts accumulated while they were at sea. (Also see Mariner.)

Landlubber—"Lubber" is an old slang term for a stupid person. This nautical term refers to a person who is uncomfortable afloat or ignorant about boats, but not to someone who has studied *Captain Bucko's Nauti-Words Handbook!*

Landsman—If a man had been pressed into service aboard a warship, that vessel's boatswain first evaluated their skills to determine what their duties aboard might be. A person with no experience at sea may be classified as a landsman, and assigned general "housekeeping" tasks on board. (Also see Boatswain and Pressed Into Service.)

Larboard—This infrequently used term is a contraction of "leaning board," and was once used to mean a vessel's left side. To avoid further confusion with the term starboard, by 1846 both the British and the American navies had adopted the term "port." (Also see Port [Side] and Starboard [Side].)

Lateen—This is the nautical term for a triangular sail suspended from a boom that runs diagonal to the mast. (Also see Mast.)

Lay—This nautical term is most commonly used: (1) to direct a person to go somewhere, e.g., "Lay aft!" or "Lay aloft!" but it is also used (2) to describe the direction in which the strands of a rope are twisted, e.g., from right to left, or (3) to describe the ability of a close hauled sailing vessel to reach a given point. (Also see Rope.)

Lazarette—This is the term for a storage compartment in the stern of a vessel, but it apparently came from back when Italian cities suffering plagues or epidemics would keep their diseased on quarantine vessels called *lazarettos*. In those days, ship's Masters often kept small arms, money, or important papers in small chests in their after cabins, which were off limits to the crew. Over time these "quarantined" chests became known as *lazarettes*, a term now used for any lockable storage compartment in the after part of a vessel. (Also see Cabin, Crew, Master, and Stern.)

League—While this unit of distance varies a bit, in England a nautical league equals about three and a half miles. With all due respect to Jules Verne, if one were actually "20,000 Leagues Under The Sea," they would no longer be on this planet!

Learning The Ropes—This phrase for becoming familiar with a new job originated in the days when no two sailing vessels had identical rigging. Even sister ships that were rigged by the same rigger were different after several repairs. When new crewmen joined a vessel it may take them a week before they "learned the ropes," and even old hands could require several days to do so. (Also see Knows The Ropes, Rope, and Ship.)

Lee—This nautical term refers to the side of something that is sheltered from the wind.

Lee Shore—This phrase refers to the shore toward which the wind blows. Prudent mariners make it a habit to stay well off a lee shore in a storm, because *Murphy's Law* always applies. (Also see Lee and Mariner.)

Leeward—This nautical term refers to the direction with the wind, i.e., downwind. Leeward is the opposite of windward. (Also see Windward.)

Leeway—This term refers to the lateral movement of a vessel or an object that is caused by wind or current. One of the functions of a keel in sailing vessels is to reduce leeway. (Also see Keel.)

Let The Cat Out Of The Bag—The cat o' nine tails was kept in a bag, and it was not taken out until the offender had been secured and there was no chance for a last-minute reprieve. (Also see Cat O' Nine Tails and Secure.)

Lighter—This is a name given a typically broad-beamed, flat-bottomed boat used to transport cargo between an offshore vessel and the land. The term "lighter" denotes such a vessel used for short distance operations, whereas "barges" were used for longer distance transfers. (Also see Boat.)

Like A Dog Wetting The Snow—This picturesque nautical phrase refers to a snake-like wake that is characteristic of a poor helmsman (and more than a few recreational boaters). (Also see Wake.)

Limey—This nickname for the British came from the fact that Royal Navy ships were required to carry a supply of limejuice to prevent scurvy (and for flavoring their daily grog). (Also see Grog and Ship.)

Line—This is the nautical term for cordage that is applied for a specific purpose aboard a vessel. Traditionally, onboard cordage that has not been put to a use is still called rope. (Also see Aboard and Rope.)

List—This term refers to the leaning over of a vessel because of excess weight on one side. (Also see Careen and Heel.)

Little Nipper—This term originated from the days when messenger lines were used to lead a vessel's main anchor cable onto the capstan being turned by her crewmen. The lashing line that was used to attach the messenger was called a "nipper," and the knot used was called a "nip." While the men turned the capstan, ship's boys would scurry beneath their feet tending to the lashing lines as the anchor cable was hauled aboard. They became known as "little nippers." (Also see Capstan and Messenger.)

Load Lines—This nautical term refers to lines or marks painted upon the sides of a vessel to indicate how low she can safely rest in the water. These could be fairly important!

Lobscouse—This was just one name that sailors called a stew of potatoes, onions, salted meat, broken pieces of hardtack, and whatever spices might make it taste better. Where's that Gamay Beaujolais! (Also see Hardtack.)

Log Book—This strange name for an official record book comes from the days when a vessel's records were written upon shingles that were cut from logs. Holes were drilled in them, they were  bound with leather thongs, and they were quite surprisingly called "log books." What a clever name! (Figure Courtesy of the US Navy)

Lollywater—This is a relatively recent nautical term for soft drinks, soda pop, etc. (Also see Geedunk.)

Long Shot—This phrase for an unlikely occurrence actually originated back when early shipboard cannons were so inaccurate that only very lucky shots would hit their marks at any great distance.

Loose Cannon—These days this phrase is used to refer to a person who is unpredictable or out of control. Aboard vessels that carried cannons it was important to make sure they were very well secured, since objects weighing several tons can do a lot of damage. When heavy weather was expected crews lashed the big guns down, and during battle they were restrained to prevent the recoil from sending them backwards across the deck. (Also see Aboard, Deck, and Secure.)

Lord Of The Plank—Long before the "Lord of the Rings" ever came along, this nautical phrase was used by crewmembers to refer to the Officer Of The Deck aboard their vessels. (Also see Officer Of The Deck.)

Lubber—This is a nautical term for a stupid, clumsy, or unskilled individual. (Also see Landlubber and Landsman.)

Lubber's Line—This phrase refers to a permanent line or mark on a compass that indicates (when it is properly installed) the direction that is forward and parallel to the vessel's keel.

Lucky Bag—This nautical term actually refers to a place where lost and found items were kept. The items were periodically returned to their owners, along with three strokes from the cat o' nine tails just to remind them not to lose things! (Also see Cat O' Nine Tails.)

Lumper—This is the slang term for a person hired to: (1) take a vessel from one port to another, or (2) unload a vessel in a port. The nickname came from the fact that such individuals were often paid a "lump sum" for their services.

M

Main Deck—This is the term that is used to denote the uppermost complete deck of a vessel. (Also see Deck.)

Main Mast—This generally refers to the tallest mast upon a sailing vessel. The main mast might be the most forward mast as on a ketch or a yawl, or one furthest aft as on a schooner. (Also see Aft, Forward, Ketch, Mast, Schooner, and Yawl.)

Mainsail—This term is used to denote the principal sail that is set on a vessel's main mast. (Also see Main Mast.)

Mainsheet—This nautical term refers to the line that controls the angle of a vessel's mainsail. (Also see Mainsail and Sheet.)

Mainstay—While this term is currently used to refer to folks upon whom others depend, e.g., "They are a mainstay of our organization!" it originally meant the stay extending from foot of the foremast to the maintop. (Also see Stay and Foremast.)

Main Topsail—This term is used to refer to a topsail that is located on a vessel's main mast. (Also see Main Mast.)

Make Fast—This nautical term means to attach a line to something in order to secure it. (Also see Fast, Line, and Secure.)

Making Way—This is the nautical term used to denote that a vessel is actually moving through the water. Note that a vessel can be underway, but not making way. (Also see Underway.)

Manila—This was the term used for rot-resistant natural fiber cordage that was found aboard many vessels before synthetic fibers became available. The name reflects the fact that much of it came from the Philippines.

Manning The Yards—This nautical custom began centuries ago, when the crewmen of a square-rigger would stand along her yards and atop her masts to give three cheers as a ceremonial salute to a distinguished person. The custom evolved into standing at their vessel's rails, which is a lot more common (and much less precarious). Today, manning the rails (or yards) is often done to honor heads of state and when a vessel returns home from deployment. It can be a stirring sight that can make even old Captain Bucko a little bit misty, but when is the next flogging? (Also see Dressing Ship, Mast, Passing Honors, Passing With Flying Colors, Square-Rigger, and Yard.)

Marina—This term refers to a facility that provides long-term and/or temporary moorings and other marine services, e.g., fuel, pump outs, maintenance. (Also see Mooring.)

Mariner—Technically this term denotes somebody who is employed in a sea-going vessel.

Mark Twain—Way back when Samuel Clemens was a riverboat pilot, this phrase indicated a sounding of two fathoms. It still does. (Also see Fathom and Pilot.)

Marlinspike—This nautical term refers to another tool that is used to open the strands of a rope or line for splicing. (Also see Fid, Line, and Rope.)

Marlinspike Sailor—This is the nautical term for an individual who is skilled at working with canvas and lines, e.g., knots, splicing. Marlinspike skills are getting rare these days. (Also see Line.)

Marooned—The term actually stems from the plight of the Ci-maroon Indians, who were brought to the West Indies by Spaniards as slave labor then left there to starve. Marooning was a common punishment for mutineers, who sometimes were left on an island with a cutlass, a musket, and a flask of water…and sometimes without anything whatsoever. (Also see Cutlass and Mutiny.)

Marrying The Gunner's Daughter—This phrase was used to describe the predicament of someone who was being flogged while they were strapped across the barrel of one of the ship's cannons. (Also see Over The Barrel.)

Massachusetts Sleigh Ride—This was how whalers referred to being towed behind their quarries by lines attached to their harpoon. This is also sometimes called a Narragansett Sleigh Ride.

Mast—This is the term for the vertical spar(s) or pole(s) on a sailing vessel that support(s) her sails, booms, etc. On power vessels, masts are used for mounting antennas, lights, etc. (Also see Spar.)

Master—This is a proper title for the licensed head of a non-military vessel. However, it has become traditional to call a licensed Master of a commercial or pleasure vessel "Captain." (Also see Captain.)

Master At Arms—This title actually stems from the days when the Royal Navy employed "Sea Corporals," to keep order and to maintain a vessel's small arms. Such individuals were trained in hand-to-hand fighting methods, and truly were "masters at arms." (Also see Jaunty.)

Mate—This is the title for a deck officer who ranks below the Master. A vessel's First, Second, and Third, Mates each have a specific set of (traditional) responsibilities. (Also see Master and Officer.)

Matthew Walker—This was supposedly the name of a British rigger in the 1800s that got into trouble and was locked up until he invented a knot that his jailor could not tie or untie.

Mayday!—This internationally recognized distress call for immediately life-threatening circumstances came from the French word *m'aidez,* which means, "Help me." Please!

McNamara's Lace—This phrase refers to the fancy work, e.g., macramé, that sailors created during their off-duty hours at sea. It apparently began with an old boatswain who had too much time on his hands in between floggings. (Also see Boatswain.)

Mess—This refers to the space(s) in a vessel where meals are eaten. It comes from the French word *mes* that means a portion of food, and it does not necessarily refer to the condition of such spaces. (Also see Crew's Mess and Officer's Mess.)

Messenger—This is a nautical term for a light line that may be thrown, lead through tight places, or otherwise manipulated to guide or to pull a heavier line. (Also see Heaving Line and Line.)

Minding One's Ps and Qs—Today this phrase is often offered as advice to be on one's best behavior, but it originated back when sailors drank on credit at waterfront taverns until they got paid. The tavern owners kept track of the Pints (Ps) and Quarts (Qs) that each sailor had consumed, while the sailors attempted to keep track of the tavern owner's accounting.

Missing The Boat—Now days this phrase refers to letting an opportunity escape, but it originally referred to missing the boat that took a sailor on shore liberty back to his ship. (Also see Boat.)

Mizzenmast—This is the nautical term used for the aftermost mast of a sailing vessel. (Also see Mast.)

Monkey—From the 1500s through the 1700s, this was the nautical slang for almost anything that was relatively small in size. A *monkey fist* was a small knot in a heaving line, a *monkey jacket* was a short coat, a *monkey pump* was a hollow quill or straw sailors used to surreptitiously drink from a coconut or cask, *powder monkeys* were ship's boys who carried gunpowder during battles, and even small coastal trading vessels were sometimes called "monkeys." (Also see Heaving Line, Monkey Fist, Monkey Jacket, and Powder Monkeys.)

Monkey Fist—This phrase has nothing to do with a gesture made by an angry simian. It refers to a heavy knot often tied in an end of a heaving line to make it much easier to throw. (Also see Heaving Line.)

Monkey Jacket—This was a nickname that sailors gave to a thick jacket they sometimes wore while standing watches at night or during foul weather.

Mooncusser—This was the slang name for nefarious folks who lured vessels onto rocks and shoals during nights when there was no illuminating moonlight. (Also see Jibber The Kibber.)

Moonraker—Apologies to James Bond, but this term initially referred to a lightweight square sail that might be set above the skysail on square-rigged vessels during fair weather. (Also see Skyscraper.)

Moor—This nautical term refers to securing a vessel to a fixed object, mooring buoy, etc. (Also see Mooring and Secure.)

Mooring—This term refers to a facility provided for securing a vessel in the above manner. (Also see Moor and Secure.)

Mud Pilot—This is the name that deep-water sailors sometimes use for a freshwater pilot who navigates visually and without sounding information. (Also see Pilot.)

Muster—This nautical term means to assemble a vessel's crew and/or passengers. (Also see Crew.)

Mutiny—While most agree this refers to a forceful resistance or revolt against established authority, it may also be simply a refusal to obey a legal order of a superior officer. (Also see Hang From The Yards, Keelhauling, and Marooning.)

N

Nautical Mile—This unit of distance is roughly 6076 feet, or about 1.125 statute miles.

Neptune—This is the name of the Roman's chief god of the sea. (Also see Poseidon and Otho's Beard.)

Neptune's Sheep—Because sheep rarely swim very far from land, this must be the nautical phrase for the patches of white foam created by waves breaking in deep water. (Also see Neptune.)

No Great Shakes—When barrels or casks became empty, they were "shaken" (taken apart) so that the staves (shakes) could be stored in a smaller space on board. Such shakes had little value.

No Man's Land—This has come to mean any dangerous or undesirable place, but it once referred to that area between the aft end of the forecastle and the forward end of a vessel's booms where lines, blocks, and tackle were often stowed. (Also see Aft, Forecastle, Forward, Line, Stowing, and Tackle.)

No Quarter—This phrase stills means to show no mercy, and it once actually indicated a fight to the death. It means the opposite of "giving quarter," an old custom by which officers might be able to save their lives by surrendering one quarter of their pay. (Also see Officer and Quarter.)

No Room To Swing A Cat—Before PETA gets upset, you ought to know that this phrase comes from the days when all hands were called on deck to witness punishments. On vessels with large crews, this could result in such a crowd the cat o' nine tails could not be swung. It seemed to occur more frequently whenever the victim was popular with the rest of the crew. (Also see Cat O' Nine Tails, Crew, and Deck.)

Norwegian Steam—This is the slang expression for good old-fashioned muscle power. So weigh that anchor, Olaf!

Now You're Talking—Even this phrase has a nautical origin. When her sails were properly set and a vessel was well balanced, crewmembers may complement her by saying, "Now you're talking!"

O

Oakum—This was the name used for the tarred fibers made from old and condemned ropes that had been picked apart. Oakum was often used to caulk the seams of early wooden vessels. (Also see Between The Devil and The Deep and Rope.)

Off And On—This phrase that we use to mean "occasionally" or "now and then," came from an expression for staying close to the shore by sailing *off* (away from) and *on* (towards) shore.

Officer—This term could refer to: (1) any licensed member of a ship's company, or (2) a person holding a commission in one of the military services. (Also see Ship's Company.)

Officer Of the Deck—This refers to the officer on deck as the Captain's representative during a particular watch. (Also see Captain and Lord Of The Plank.)

Officer's Mess—This phrase denotes the dining facility for a vessel's officers, which may be separate from those for her passengers and the rest of her crew. (Also see Crew and Mess.)

Old Salt—This is the nautical term used for an experienced and/or well-seasoned mariner. (Also see Mariner, Sea Dog, and Shellback.)

One Good Turn Deserves Another—This phrase actually evolved from nautical advice to keep a vessel (or anything of value) secure by taking another turn of its lines around mooring bitts. (Also see Line, Mooring, and Secure.)

Opportunity—Large ships often depended on an incoming tide to enter certain ports, and if they arrived too early or late they had to stand off and wait for the next flood tide. Early Roman sailors called this *ob portu*, which meant, "standing off port, waiting the right moment." Over time, this phrase evolved into the modern English word "opportunity."

Ordinary Seaman—This is the title given an apprentice able bodied seaman, and it is also used for the lowest rank among members of a vessel's deck crew. (Also see Able Bodied Seaman.)

Otho's Beard—Otho was the Irish equivalent of Neptune, and this was what Irish sailors call breaking waves. *Trivial Tidbit*—Irish legend says all sea creatures came from Otho's Beard. (Also see Neptune.)

Outboard—This term refers to a position that is toward, or beyond, a vessel's sides. It is also used to refer to an engine that is mounted outside the main hull, often on the transom. (Also see Transom.)

Outdrive—This relatively new nautical term is used to describe the outboard portion of an Inboard/Outboard (I/O) propulsion system. It is also sometimes referred to as a "stern drive." (Also see Outboard and Stern Drive.)

Outrigger—This is a general term for a structure that extends beyond the side of a vessel's hull for a special purpose. Fishing boats may use outriggers to spread their lines, while Polynesian canoes sometimes use outriggers to support a small secondary hull.

Overboard—Since the planking on a vessel's sides was once known as her "boards," this refers to something being over the side, or outside, of a vessel. (Also see By The Boards, Outboard, and Planking.)

Overhand Knot—This basic knot is tied by passing a line's end around its standing part. (Also see Bend, Bight, and Line.)

Overhead—This is roughly the nautical equivalent of the term "ceiling" that is used in buildings ashore. (Also see Ceiling.)

Over-Reach—This term is currently used when someone goes too far or is overextended, but it originally referred to a sailing vessel staying on a tack too long to reach a desired position. (Also see Tack.)

Over The Barrel—Today we use this phrase to denote being in a difficult position with relatively few alternatives, but it once meant something a lot worse. To be flogged, a subject might be tied to a mast, grating, or over the barrel of one of the vessel's cannons by its deck rings. (Also see Cat O' Nine Tails, Combing The Cat, and Marrying The Gunner's Daughter.)

Overwhelm—The modern definition of this word is "overpower" or "swallow up," but it came from a nautical term that means to capsize or founder, neither of which is good. (Also see Founder.)

P

Packing Gland—This does not have anything to do with irregular body functions, but is a nautical term for the fitting where a vessel's propeller shaft and/or rudderstock passes through her hull. Sometimes also called a "stuffing box," it is designed both to provide lubrication and to prevent leaks. (Also see Stuffing Box.)

Painter—This is the nautical term for a line at the stem of a boat that is used to secure or tow it. (Also see Boat, Line, Secure, and Stem.)

Pass Down The Line—Although this nautical phrase originally referred to relaying a signal from one vessel to the next one astern in a column, today it simply means to "pass it on." (Also see Astern.)

Passing Honors—Passing honors may be rendered when Navy or Coast Guard vessels pass close aboard, e.g., 600 yards for ships, 400 yards for boats. When this is done, "Attention" is ordered and a hand salute given by all individuals in view on deck and not in ranks. (Also see Boat, Deck, Hand Salutes, and Passing With Flying Colors.)

Passing With Flying Colors—Now days this phrase is used to mean that somebody has met a personal challenge or test with excellent marks, but it came from the custom of sailing vessels flying their colors (flags) as they passed other vessels. (Also see Passing Honors.)

Pass The Word—This nautical phrase means to repeat something to other members of a vessel's crew. (Also see Crew.)

Pay Out—This nautical term means to feed out a line, hand over hand. (Also see Line.)

Pea Coat—This heavy topcoat worn by sailors was once made from Pilot cloth, a heavy type of blue-twilled cloth with nap on one side. Such fabric was sometimes called P-cloth for the first letter of the term "Pilot." The garment was called a "P-coat," which over the years evolved into today's Pea Coat.

Perks—This term was not invented by, or for, yuppies. It is a contraction of "perquisites," which referred to the allowances in money or kind that were given with a naval appointment or office.

Pieces Of Eight—This slang term referred to Spanish silver pesos of the 1600s and 1700s which were worth eight *Reales*, and were marked with the number eight on one side. Sometimes these coins would be cut into eight parts, each worth one *Real*...hence the term "pieces of eight."

Pier—This is a nautical term for a vessel landing/loading platform that extends at an angle from the shore. *Trivial Tidbit*—The "foot" of a pier is at its shoreward end, while its "head" is offshore.

Pilot—Some areas, e.g., rivers, harbors, canals, require that vessels be guided by a licensed pilot who has specific local knowledge and is qualified to navigate vessels through those areas. Pilots usually board a vessel to assist her Captain or Master with navigation, etc. outside such areas, and remain aboard until the vessel is clear of the area or at her mooring. (Also see Captain, Master, and Mooring.)

Pipe Down—This phrase originally referred to the boatswain's pipe call given upon completion of an all hands task as the signal that crewmembers that were not on watch could go below. It was also the last call each day, in which case it meant to stop talking and remain silent. (Also see Below Deck, Boatswain's Pipe, and Watches.)

Piping Hot—This term originated back when boatswain's pipes signaled that the ship's meals were ready and (hopefully even) still warm, e.g., piping hot. (Also see Boatswain's Pipe.)

Pirate—There are important distinctions among true pirates, buccaneers, and privateers. The true pirates stole from anyone purely for their own gain. One of the most feared pirates was Edward Teach, more commonly known as *Blackbeard*. He was said to have braided pieces of rope into his hair and lit them during battle, just to look more terrifying. If the sight of this did not frighten his opponents, the smell probably would! (Also see Buccaneer, Privateers, and Rope.)

Pitching—This nautical term refers to the see-saw movements of a vessel's bow and stern, as they are alternately lifted by the passing wave crests only to fall into their following troughs. (Also see Bow and Stern.)

Pitch poling—This term refers to when a vessel is thrown end-over-end in heavy seas. This is not something to do regularly!

Planing—This is the term for a condition in which a vessel's hull is lifted by hydrodynamic and/or aerodynamic forces so that it rides with only twenty-five percent or less of its surface area in the water, to perhaps reach a speed that is greater than that achievable by vessels with displacement hulls. (Also see Displacement Hull and Planing Hull.)

Planing Hull—This refers to a type of hull that is specifically designed to plane with the application of sufficient power and speed. (Also see Displacement Hull, Planing, and Planing Speed.)

Planing Speed—This term is used to describe the minimum speed at which a vessel with a planing hull will come onto plane and will remain on plane. (Also see Planing and Planing Hull.)

Planking—This is the general term for the boards used to cover the ribs, frames, deck or hull of a wooden vessel. *Trivial Tidbit*—The equivalent for steel-hulled vessels is called plating. (Also see Board.)

Plank Owner—If you were on a vessel's commissioning crew and served aboard her for at least a year, tradition said you were entitled to a plank from her deck when she was decommissioned. However, it is getting a lot more difficult to find such planks aboard today's steel and plastic vessels.

Pollywog—This is the nautical term used for an inexperienced mariner who has not yet crossed the equator aboard a vessel. (Also see Crossing The Line, Mariner, and Shellback.)

Poop Deck—This nautical phrase refers to a partial deck at a vessel's stern above her main deck. The name actually has nothing to do with onboard sanitary facilities, but actually evolved from when early Mediterranean sailors carried sacred idols on their vessels' sterns. Romans called their idols *puppis*, and that after part of their vessels was called a *puppim*. Over time, *puppim* evolved into *poupe*, and finally into poop deck. But this rather lengthy explanation has left me pooped! (Also see Aft, Deck, Main Deck, Pooped, and Stern.)

Pooped—Now days we use this word to indicate that one is exhausted, but it evolved from the days when large sailing vessels had a raised poop deck aft. If a vessel's stern got overtaken by following seas, she was said to have been "pooped." So what else were you expecting? (Also see Aft, Following Seas, Poop Deck, and Stern.)

Port Holes—King Henry VI of England insisted upon cannons for his ship that were too big to be mounted in the more traditional ways, e.g., in the forecastle. Doors were cut into the vessel's side and her cannons located below deck. The phrase evolved into meaning any opening in a vessel's side (even if your boat does not have all that many  of those pesky big cannons). (Also see Below Deck, Boat, and Forecastle.) (Figure Courtesy of the US Navy)

Port (Side)—In earlier times the left side of a vessel (facing forward) was called larboard, and her right side was referred to as starboard. But because these two terms sounded too similar when shouted over the noise aboard ship, sailors started using the word "port," which actually referred to the opening on the vessel's left side through which cargo was transferred. The Royal Navy officially adopted the term "port" in 1844, to be followed by the US Navy in 1846. (Also see Larboard and Starboard [Side].)

Poseidon—This was the name of Greek's god of the sea. After all, the Romans had Neptune and the Irish had Otho. (Also see Neptune and Otho's Beard.)

POSH—When wealthy Britishers cruised between England and India, the most comfortable, i.e., cooler, cabins were on a vessel's port (side) on the outbound trip and on her starboard (side) when homeward bound. These cabins were in such high demand that only extremely wealthy passengers would have the letters "P.O.S.H." (Port Out Starboard Home) written adjacent to their names in the reservation books. Now days we still use this term to indicate luxurious accommodations. (Also see Port [Side] and Starboard [Side].)

Pouring Oil On Troubled Waters—Today we use this to mean trying to relieve tense situations, but it originally referred to an old (before the Exxon Valdez) practice of releasing oil in heavy weather to calm the seas.

Powder Monkeys—This was a nickname given to ship's boys who carried gunpowder and water. (Also see Monkey.)

Pressed Into Service—Now days this phrase is used to indicate that one was told or coerced into doing some unpleasant job, but it stems from days when press gangs recruited men to serve aboard ships. (Also see Press Gang.)

Press Gang—Press gangs were legally sanctioned as far back as the 1200s, and the Royal Navy relied quite heavily upon this method of "recruiting" until the 1830s. With few exceptions, any man between the ages of 18 and 55 could be pressed into service in this way. The last law passed on the practice said that a pressed man could not be required to serve for over five years, and could not be impressed for a second time. But press gangs have never been officially abolished, so the practice is still legal today. Stay out of those dark alleys in England! (Also see Pressed Into Service.)

Privateer—These individuals held a Government's sanction to bear arms against named enemies, and were (usually) exempt from punishment. Henry Morgan was once a privateer for England, and so was Captain Kidd…whom they later hung as a pirate. Hey, I did say "usually!" (Also see Pirate.)

Privileged vessel—This nautical phrase refers to a vessel that, according to the applicable navigation Rules of the Road, should have the right of way over a burdened (or a give-way) vessel, and should maintain her current course and speed. (Also see Burdened Vessel, Give-Way Vessel, Stand-On Vessel, and Rules Of The Road.)

Proof—This expression evolved from the way that customs officers once checked the alcohol content of rum at dockside by pouring a small amount into a dish and attempting to light it. If it was at least fifty percent alcohol by volume it would ignite and was declared to be "up to proof," and that is why today 100-proof liquor is still defined as about fifty percent alcohol by volume.

Prow—This is the nautical term that is used for the portion of a vessel's bow that is forward of, and above, her waterline. (Also see Bow, Forward, and Waterline.)

Pulpit—Sorry Reverend, but this nautical term refers to an elevated rail structure at a vessel's bow. (Also see Bow and Pushpit.)

Punt—Besides being a fourth-down option in football, this is the nautical term for a small flat-bottomed boat that is square at both ends. A punt may not be as cute as a dinghy or a dink, but it is definitely cuter than most scows. (Also see Boat, Dinghy, Dink, and Scow.)

Purser—This is the title given an officer aboard a passenger or merchant vessel that is in charge of accounts, etc. Imagine a nautical bean-counter.

Purser Rigged And Parish Damned—This was the slang phrase used to describe individuals who enlisted in the Navy simply because they were too poor to do anything else. (Also see Purser.)

Pushpit—This infrequently used nautical term refers to an elevated rail structure at a vessel's stern. (Also see Pulpit and Stern.)

Pussy Whipped—The nautical origin for this phrase actually dates back to when some vessels used a lesser version of the cat o' nine tails to discipline younger crew members. Such a whip typically had only five flails, and was called a "pussy." (Also see Cat O' Nine Tails.)

Putting A New Slant On Things—Now days this phrase is used to mean viewing a problem from a different perspective, but it came from the fact that all sailing vessels have an optimum angle of heel (leaning over). If one begins to exceed that angle, it is often better to reduce sail rather than spill the wind and lose power. In other words, it is time to "put a new slant on things."

Putting One's Oar In—This nautical expression means to interfere in somebody else's business. In other words, if you are not rowing the boat keep your oar out of the water!

Q

Quarter—This term refers to those portions of a vessel's sides that are forward of her stern, and abaft her beam. Quartering winds or seas bear 45 degrees abaft of the beam, and vessels have both port and starboard quarters. *Trivial Tidbit*—The phrase "Giving Quarter" actually refers to a custom by which officers might be able save their lives by surrendering one quarter of their pay. (Also see Abaft, Beam, No Quarter, Officer, Port [Side], Starboard [Side], and Stern.)

Quarterdeck—This term refers to that portion of a vessel's deck just abaft the main mast (or the same general location on vessels without main masts) that is typically reserved for officers. (Also see Abaft, Deck, Main Mast, and Officer.)

Quay—This is a nautical term for a structure along the edge of a harbor that is frequently used for the loading/offloading of cargo or embarkation/debarkation of passengers. (Also see Debark, Embark, and Wharf.)

R

Rafting Up—This nautical term refers to when two or more vessels tie up alongside each other to exchange important scuttlebutt, consume tasty tidbits and frosty beverages, etc. (Also see Alongside and Scuttlebutt.)

Ready About—This nautical expression is used to advise/warn those aboard a sailing vessel that she is about to come about or to change to a different tack. (Also see Come About, Hard Alee, and Tack.)

Red Right Returning—This is the old saying often used to remember to keep red buoys, etc. on one's right when entering a harbor, channel, etc., heading upstream, or generally going from a larger body of water to a smaller one. But as with most old sayings, there are always exceptions!

Reefing—This nautical term has nothing to do with running aground or even with smoking funny cigarettes. It refers to taking in some of a vessel's sail to reduce her sail area. (Also see Reef Lines.)

Reef Lines—This can mean a shallow offshore area where a reef comes close to the surface, but it is also the nautical term for the short pieces of line used for reefing the sails. (Also see Line and Reefing.)

Repel Boarders!—This was an order given to the ship's company to defend their vessel from boarders. It still comes in handy if yours is the only vessel rafted up that has frosty beverages. (Also see Rafting Up and Ship's Company.)

Revenue Cutter—This is the general name given to a single-mast cutter specifically built for the prevention of smuggling and enforcement of customs regulations. (Also see Cutter.)

Riding The Spanish Mare—This nautical phrase refers to another method of shipboard punishment. If the victim stayed astride a boom with its stay slackened-off for the allotted time period while the vessel was at sea, they were released. But if they fell off, they likely drowned. (Also see Stay.)

Rise And Shine—This phrase evolved out of the old awakening call, "Rouse and shine!" which was gently whispered in sailors' ears every morning by the vessel's boatswain. (Also see Boatswain.)

Rocks And Shoals—This is the slang term that sailors sometimes use when they are referring to US Navy Regulations.

Rode—This is the nautical term used to refer to the line and/or chain attached to a vessel's anchor. (Also see Ground Tackle and Line.)

Rogue Knot—This is the nautical term for a knot that is tied upside down. It is sometimes called a "granny knot," and might not hold very well if under strain.

Rope—Traditionally, this term is used for cordage as it is purchased or stowed, but some use this term for cordage that is larger than an inch in diameter. When rope is put to use aboard a vessel, it is referred to as line. (Also see Line.)

Rope Yarn Sunday—This expression refers to a relaxed work schedule when crewmembers that were not on watch were allowed to tend to personal matters, etc.

Round Robin—Although it is typically used today with regard to sports tournaments, this phrase actually originated back when British mutineers signed their names in circles so that their leaders could not be identified. Those limeys were sneaky blokes!

Rules Of The Road—This is the nautical term used for the sets of navigational rules governing the right-of-way when there may be a possibility of collision, etc., among two or more vessels. Although the cabin cruiser in the adjacent photograph had the right-of-way, it appears that somebody neglected to inform the skipper of the run-about before he rammed her. In spite of this, note that both vessels are still floating! (Also see Skipper.) (Photograph Courtesy of the US Coast Guard)

Rummage Sale—This common expression was partially derived from the French word *arrimage*, which means a vessel's cargo. In those days, damaged cargo was often sold at a "rummage sale."

Running The Gauntlet—This phrase came from a method of military punishment that was prominent in the early 1600s. On board ships, offenders were forced to pass between lines of crewmen who would beat them with knotted ropes, whips, or clubs. Not a pleasant experience!

S

Sailboat—It might come as a real shock to some, but this is actually the term for a boat that uses the wind as its primary means of propulsion. Sometimes also called a "blowboat." (Also see Blow-boater and Boat.)

Sail Ho!—This is the traditional cry that was given upon sighting another sailing vessel. (Also see Where Away.)

Sailor—Although it officially once meant a crewman serving aboard a sailing vessel, these days it is more loosely used when referring to any individual who works while afloat.

Sailor's Blessing—This is a tongue-in-cheek expression for a cursing out, and sailors are famous for salty language that is often creatively enhanced with colorful expletives.

Saint Elmo's Fire—This electrical discharge that may occur in a vessel's rigging under certain atmospheric conditions, was regarded by some sailors as a good omen that signaled an end to foul weather. Conversely, others believed they would die within a day if the glow from this phenomenon fell upon their faces.

Sally Ship!—This was not the name of some waterfront floozy, but rather a command given when trying to free one's vessel that was aground or trapped in the ice. Crewmen would run back and forth from one side of their vessel to the other to try to get her rolling and broken free. Do not try this on a small boat! (Also see Aground, Boat, and Floozies.)

Saloon—Even this term has a nautical origin. When vessels began to carry paying passengers in the 1500s, they shared the officers' cabins. As the number of such passengers increased however, separate cabins became necessary. In those days, many aristocrats had rooms called "saloons" in their homes to entertain guests, so the opulently furnished cabins that were installed amidships were given the same name. During the 1800s, riverboats later took the concept westward across America, offering amenities such as gambling, liquor, and companionship for their passengers. Some of their passengers settled ashore and built their own saloons, and the rest as they say…is history. (Also see Amidships, Cabin, and Officer.)

Schooner—This comes from the words *schoon* or *scoon* that meant to move smoothly and quickly. It is actually not one specific type of vessel, but rather refers to fore-and-aft rigged sailing vessels having between two and six masts. However, a two-mast vessel with only a main mast and a mizzenmast is not con-

Schooner

sidered to be a schooner. Three-mast schooners were common, but those with five, six, or even seven masts were so hard to handle they were called man-killers (square riggers were much safer). *Trivial Tidbit*—Barquentines, Brigantines, and Hermaphrodite Brigs all belong to the schooner family. (Also see Barquentine, Brig, Brigantine, Fore-And-Aft, Main Mast, Mast, and Mizzenmast.) (Figure Courtesy of J. Wilkinson)

Scow—This picturesque term refers to a boat with a flat bottom and square ends. Lovely! (Also see Punt.)

Scraping The Bottom Of The Barrel—Although we currently use this phrase to mean a "last choice," it came from when ship's cooks would literally scrape the bottoms of barrels to get the last of the pork fat. This was often secreted away by the ship's cooks to be later sold ashore to tanneries, chandleries, etc. (Also see Chandlery and Slush Fund.)

Scrimshaw—This nautical term refers to the carving or etching mariners did on bones, teeth, tusks, or shells.

Scuppers—This nautical term refers to holes cut through a vessel's sides to drain water from her deck(s). (Also see Deck.)

Scuttle—This term is used for a small opening or hatch on deck, but it was originally the nautical word for cutting a hole in something, like a keg or even a vessel's hull. This term also means to intentionally sink a vessel by doing the latter. (Also see Deck, Hatch, and Scuttlebutt.)

Scuttlebutt—This term was the result of combining the nautical word "scuttle" (that means to make a hole in something), and "butt" (the name given a keg that held about 126 gallons of drinking water). A Scuttlebutt was originally such a keg with a hole chopped into it so that crewmen could dip out drinking water, but the term was later also applied to  a drinking fountain. Some maintain that this term was used to refer to a small ladle with holes (scuttles) cut into it so that the crew would not spend too much time in idle conversation. Because gossip frequently began around the scuttlebutt, this term is now used to denote rumors. (Also see Crew and Scuttle.) (Figure Courtesy of the US Navy)

Sea Anchor—This is a device that might be used to reduce a vessel's drift, reduce her speed, and/or hold her bow into the sea during heavy weather conditions. (Also see Bow and Drogue.)

Sea Breeze—This is the term for an onshore wind that often occurs as the air over the land heats up, rises, and draws in the (cooler) offshore air. (Also see Land Breeze.)

Sea Cock—This is not a nautical rooster, but rather a valve on a through-hull pipe or fitting. If you open these at the wrong time, see Scuttle.

Sea Dog—This was a slang term for an Elizabethan privateer, but it is also sometimes used to refer to a well-seasoned and experienced mariner. (Also see Mariner, Old Salt, Privateer, and Shellback.)

Sea Lawyer—This is a name (not so affectionately) used for an argumentative person, or somebody who routinely tries to apply rules and regulations to their personal advantage.

Seamanship—This term refers collectively to the combined arts and skills of: rigging, marlinspike work, sail handling, piloting, the operation and maintenance of a vessel, etc. (Also see Pilot and Marlinspike.)

Sea Room—This is a nautical term for keeping a safe distance from a lee shore or other hazards. Wise mariners try to give themselves enough sea room to accommodate any unforeseen events. (Also see Lee Shore and Mariner.)

Seaworthiness—This term is used to refer to a vessel's construction, material condition, outfitting, loading, crew, training, or other factors that affect her ability to function afloat.

Secure—This nautical term means to make something fast, e.g., "Secure that line!" (Also see Fast and Make Fast.)

Sextant—This is a navigational instrument used to measure the altitudes and angular distances of celestial bodies. It is also sometimes referred to by the slang term "horse's leg."

Shake A Leg—This phrase is currently used to mean get up and get out of bed, but it originated back in the days when women were allowed to stay onboard during longer in-port periods. Every morning, the boatswain would come into the crew's berthing area and call out, "Show-a-leg!" If a man's leg appeared he had to get up and start working, whereas a woman was allowed to sleep in. The phrase "show a leg" turned into "shake a leg," until the practice of letting women stay onboard was abolished in 1840. (Also see Berth and Boatswain.)

Shanghaied—Now days we use this term to indicate that one is forced to do something against their will, but it originated back when it was so difficult to get sailors to sign aboard for long or otherwise arduous voyages that ship owners and/or Masters had to be somewhat "creative." Men who had been drugged or knocked unconscious may awaken to find they were en route to remote ports like Shanghai. In other cases, local authorities may suggest that known troublemakers be "shipped to Shanghai" just to get rid of them for a while. (Also see Hijack and Master.)

Shape Up—Today this phrase is used to mean "pull yourself together" or to improve your physical condition, e.g., eat right, exercise daily, die anyway, but it originally referred to how a vessel off a lee shore would "shape up" her course to lessen the danger of going aground. (Also see Aground and Lee.)

Sheepshank—When you get finished "shanking sheep," you might want to consider using this nautical knot to non-destructively shorten a line. (Also see Line.)

Sheet—This is the nautical term for a line that is used to set or position a vessel's sail(s) relative to the direction of the wind. (Also see Line.)

Sheet Bend—The incredibly perceptive among you might have already guessed that this bend (a nautical knot) is often used to join two sheets (lines) of unequal thickness. Captain Bucko is very impressed! (Also see Bend, Line, and Sheet.)

Shellback—This is the nautical term used for an experienced mariner who has crossed the equator aboard a vessel. (Also see Crossing The Line, Mariner, Pollywog, Old Salt, and Sea Dog.)

Ship—This term is frequently used for any vessel that is large enough to carry a boat on board. (Also see Boat.)

Shipmate—This is a nautical term that deep-water sailors use for other deep-water sailors. Even if they have not yet served in a vessel together, they still consider each other to be shipmates.

Ship's Articles—This refers to a written agreement between the Master of a vessel and her crew concerning the terms of their employment. (Also see Crew and Master.)

Ships' Bells—The use of ships' bells dates to when ships' boys kept the time using a half-hour glass. As the sand ran out, they would turn over the glass and also ring the proper number of bells. One bell was struck after the first half-hour, two bells after the first hour, three bells after an  hour and a half, etc., up to eight bells at the end of a four-hour watch. Before noon each day, the officers made observations of the sun to determine the latitude. When the sun reached its zenith, one would call out, "There he goes!" which was the signal for the ship's boy to turn over the glass and in doing so re-synchronize their vessel's time. (Also see Watches.) (Photograph Courtesy of the Naval Historical Center)

Ship's Company—This nautical term refers to persons who are employed to work in a vessel.

Shiver Me Timbers!—This expression denotes a level of surprise akin to that when a vessel is struck or strikes something with such force even her large timbers might shatter (shiver).

Shoal—This nautical term is most commonly used for a sandbar or other shallow area that might present a danger to a vessel. It may sometimes also refer to a crowd or throng of fish, people, etc.

Shot Across The Bow—When a warship wanted to stop another vessel, she might fire a cannon shot across her bow. This phrase is currently used to indicate giving a final warning.

Showing One's True Colors—The rules of war require vessels to hoist their (true) national ensigns before firing a shot, but many early warships (and most pirate vessels) carried other flags to elude or deceive enemies. They may fly one of them until an opponent came into range, then "show their true colors." This phrase still denotes deceptive practices. (Also see Bamboozle and Ensign.)

Shroud—This is the nautical term for a line or wire that supports a vessel's mast, and runs from its top to the spreaders down to the sides of the vessel. (Also see Line and Mast.)

Sickbay—Today this nautical term is commonly used to refer to a vessel's medical facility, but it originally was more of a recuperation area for the sick or wounded. The patients rested upon suspended wooden cots instead of hammocks, and the space was often scrubbed down with vinegar to reduce the spread of disease. Sickbay was not a very pleasant place. (Also see Hammocks.)

Side Boys—The old naval tradition of mustering side boys on the quarterdeck when an officer or an important person boards or departs from a vessel actually goes back to when it was common for such individuals to visit ships while they were at sea or at anchor. Because climbing a Jacob's' Ladder was rather undignified, a boatswain's chair or sling would often be used to hoist these guests over the side. The "larger" the guest the more crewmen were required for the job, and sailors began to notice that the more senior the guests were the larger they seemed to be. The tradition of piping important visitors aboard and over the side continues today, with the number of side boys being directly related to the visitor's rank or importance. (Also see Boatswain's Chair, Jacob's Ladder, Officer, and Quarterdeck.)

Sixteen Bells—Eight bells are usually the maximum number struck, but at midnight as each new year begins, eight bells are struck by the oldest member of the crew for the past year followed by another eight bells struck by the crew's youngest member for the year to come. (Also see Ship's Bells.)

Skipper—This came from the Dutch word *schipper,* which was the name used for the Master of a small trading vessel. Although it might not be as technically proper as Master or Captain, it has become generally acceptable when referring to one in charge of a vessel. (Also see Captain and Master.)

Skull And Cross Bones—The infamous Skull And Cross Bones might have flown over more Hollywood sound stages than pirate vessels, but *Blackbeard* is said to have once used such a flag with an hourglass on it to indicate that time was running out for his victims and that death was near. (Also see Blackjack and Jolly Roger.)

Skylarking—Today this old nautical term is sometimes used to mean horseplay, but it originally referred to the way young crewmen would cavort about in a vessel's rigging, defying gravity and with no apparent sense of danger. There actually once was a command for, "All hands to dance and skylark!" which could have referred to some form of physical training or was simply a way to relieve the tedium of the daily routine aboard ship. In either case, it must have been quite a sight to see.

Sky Pilot—This is the Navy nickname for a vessel's Chaplain. Could you think of a better term?

Skyscraper—This term originally referred to a small triangular sail that was set above the mainsails on old square-riggers to try to catch (scrape) a little more wind in a light breeze. Now days we use it this term for extremely tall buildings. (Also see Mainsail, Moonraker, and Square-Rigger.)

Sloop—This is the term for a sailing vessel with one mast that is fore-and-aft rigged with a single head-sail (jib or staysail) and a mainsail. If such a vessel has more than one jib however, she is often called a Cutter. (Also see Cutter, Fore-And-Aft, Jib, and Mainsail.) (Figure Courtesy of J. Wilkinson)

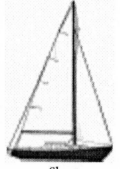

Sloop

Slop Chest—This phrase actually came from the old Middle English word *sloppe* that meant clothing, and it had nothing to do with shipboard cuisine. It referred to a chest or locker the vessel's Master maintained that contained foul weather gear, etc., he would loan to crewmen. This practice may even earn the vessel's Master a small profit for his efforts. (Also see Master.)

Slush Fund—Although we currently use this phrase to mean cash reserves or rainy day funds, it once referred to the slurry called "slush," that was obtained by scraping or by boiling the vessel's empty salted meat storage barrels. The ship's cook may sell such skimmed fat to the Purser, and it was used to make candles or protect the vessel's spars from water damage. Cooks sometimes also sold it ashore, and the money so earned became known as a "slush fund." (Also see Purser, Scraping The Bottom Of The Barrel, and Spar.)

Smelling The Ground—This nautical phrase is used to mean that a vessel's keel is nearly touching the bottom. (Also see Aground, Hard Aground, Hard And Fast, Keel, and Touch And Go.)

Smoking Lamp—Open flames are taken quite seriously aboard ship, and as smoking gained in popularity among sailors an oil burning lamp was provided to light their pipes. When the wind was blowing too strongly and/or combustible material, e.g., gunpowder, was present, smoking was not permitted. When it was safe, "The smoking lamp is lighted!" was passed to the vessel's crew. Conversely, "The smoking lamp is out!" meant to immediately cease all smoking on board.

Snotty—This rather unsavory term was originally a name that the sailors gave to lads of twelve or less who joined their first vessels as ship's boys or midshipmen. Most were too poor to afford handkerchiefs, and used their sleeves to wipe their tears and noses. To stop this habit, Lord Nelson ordered that large brass buttons be sewn upon the sleeves of all his ship's boys' and midshipmen's' uniforms. But that's enough about this rather sticky subject!

Snub—This originally meant to stop the running out of a line by taking a turn around a cleat, piling, etc.; or to slow a vessel by lowering her anchor(s). Now days we use this term to mean to ignore or avoid somebody, or to abruptly cut them off. (Also see Cleat and Line.)

So!—This was the command given to stop hauling when something had reached its desired position. So?

Soldier's Wind—This nautical phrase refers to a wind that blows hard upon a vessel's beam, so that even someone with few sailing skills, e.g., a soldier, can get her to her destination and back again. (Also see Beam.)

Sole—This nautical term is used for: (1) the interior deck of a vessel, (2) the floor of a vessel's cabin, (3) extensions of a rudder, and (4) the fiberglass deck of a sailboat's cockpit. (Also see Cabin, Deck, Floor, and Sailboat.)

Son Of A Gun—If the crew was restricted to the vessel for an extended time while in a port, women might be allowed to stay aboard. Sometimes a child was born on a vessel, and a place for this event was in between  the cannons on the vessel's gun deck. If the labor was particularly difficult, the Captain just might order a full broadside be fired during contractions to help things along. Doing this may have had some effect, because a full broadside would have been powerful enough to move the entire vessel a foot or two sideways. If a male baby's father was not known, the child was entered into the vessel's log as a "son of a gun". This was regarded as the mark of a true sailor, and it is still an offhanded compliment. (Also see Broadside, Captain, and Crew.) (Photograph Courtesy of the Naval Historical Center)

S.O.S.—Contrary to popular belief, the letters S.O.S. do not stand for "Save Our Souls" or "Save Our Ship." These three letters are simply an easily remembered and recognized signal in Morse code.

Spar—This is a long, rounded piece of wood or steel that is often tapered at one or both ends, and is part of a vessel's rigging and/or masts. (Also see Mast, Yard, and Yardarm.)

Spindrift—This nautical term refers to finely divided water particles that are blown off the crests of waves by strong winds. This was sometimes also called, "spoondrift."

Spinnaker—This is the nautical term for a large balloon-shaped and often very colorful sail. They are usually made of lightweight materials, and are sometimes also called kites or chutes.

Spinning Yarns—You might have wondered how this phrase came to mean telling stories. Before much factory-made cordage was readily available, the sailors would spin, and twist yarns into ropes themselves. This could be done while a group of them sat around telling sea stories, which as everybody knows, are always the truth. (Also see Rope and Yarn.) (Photograph by E.H. Hart Courtesy of the Naval Historical Center)

Splicing The Main Brace—A top priority after battle or heavy weather was to repair any damages to a vessel's rigging. The main brace was a heavy line that was a principal fore-and-aft support for the vessel's masts, and splicing it was one of the most difficult jobs aboard. After doing this (or any particularly arduous task), crews were often given an extra ration of grog or rum. Over the years, this phrase has evolved into being a nautical invitation to have a drink. (Also see Fore-And-Aft and Grog.)

Spring Line—This is the term for a dock line that limits a vessel's movement fore-and-aft, and may also be used as a pivot point during the processes of docking and undocking. An after bow spring line leads from a vessel's bow aft to the dock, while a forward quarter spring line leads from a vessel's quarter forward to its point of attachment on the dock. (Also see Aft, Dock, Bow, Fore-And-Aft, Forward, Line, and Quarter.)

Squared Away—Now days this term is used to compliment someone who "has their act together," but it originally referred to when the backs of the sails on a square-rigged vessel were set perpendicular to the wind to obtain the best speed.

Square Knot—This is essentially the combination of two overhand knots, and is sometimes also called a reef knot. It is frequently used to join two lines of similar size together.

Square Meal—During good weather, the vessel's crew was sometimes served (warm) food upon square wooden platters that could more easily be stowed in racks onboard. This evolved over the years into meaning any well-balanced meal.

Square Rigger—This is a generic term for a relatively large sailing vessel with three masts that had rectangular sails carried from horizontal spars or yards, set at right angles to her keel. (Also Keel, Spar, and Yard.)

Stanchion—This is the nautical term for an upright wooden or metal post used to support a vessel's railings, bulwarks, etc. (Also see Bulwarks.)

Stand By!—This was the preparatory order given to indicate that the vessel's crew should get ready for action or a command. (Also see Crew.)

Stand-On Vessel—This is another term for the vessel that should have the right-of-way in overtaking, meeting, or crossing situations, and is obliged to maintain her current course and speed. (Also see Privileged Vessel, Burdened Vessel, Give-Way Vessel, and Rules Of The Road.)

Starboard (Side)—Norsemen called the sides of their vessels "boards," and many years before rudders were invented they mounted a "steering oar" on their vessels' right sides (facing forward). The name for that side evolved into starboard and it has been so ever since. (Also see Board, Larboard, and Port [Side].)

Starting With A Clean Slate—Some insist this phrase for a new beginning came from the days when watch standers recorded their vessel's speeds, headings, distances, etc. upon a slate tablet that was kept by the helm. If there were no problems encountered during their watch, it would be wiped clean so that the oncoming watch could "start with a clean slate."

Stateroom—There is disagreement regarding the origin of this term for officer or passenger cabins. Some say it came from the 1500s and 1600s, when special cabins were reserved for statesmen.

Others maintain that the name really came from the paddlewheel steamboats that cruised the waterways of the United States during the 1800s. The first-class cabins aboard them were each named after a state in the union. In either case, the term persisted.

Stays—This term may refer to: (1) lines that run aloft from a vessel's deck to points on her mast(s) and used to support the latter, and (2) putting a sailing vessel onto a tack or to come about. (Also see Come About, Deck, Line, Mast, and Tack.)

Steady As You Go—This was a command given to a helmsman to maintain the vessel's current course and speed.

Stem—This nautical term refers to the structural member at the very front of a vessel's bow. (Also see Bow and Prow.)

Stemming The Tide—Today we use this phrase to describe overcoming adverse circumstances, but it originally referred to heading a vessel's bow directly into the current. (Also see Bow.)

Stern—This is the nautical term for a vessel's aft end, which is opposite her bow. If a vessel is making way ahead, her wake is on this end. But if she is dead in the water, do not despair. Since most vessels only have two ends, you still have a 50% chance of getting this correct. (Also see Aft, Bow, Dead In The Water, Making Way, and Wake.)

Stern Drive—This relatively new term denotes the outboard portion of an Inboard/Outboard (I/O) propulsion system. It is sometimes referred to as an "outdrive." (Also see Outboard and Outdrive.)

Stern Line—This refers to a line that leads from a vessel's stern laterally to the dock, pier, etc. Its primary function is to keep the vessel's stern alongside the dock, pier, etc. (Also Line and Stern.)

Stevedore—Despite what others might say, this is not a bullfighter named Steven. However, it is the term for a person who works with the cargo when a vessel is being loaded or unloaded in port.

Steward—If you thought that you were being pampered by having a Room Steward on your last cruise, you ought to know that this word actually came from the Saxon *stywaard*, which meant "keeper of pigs."

Stick In The Mud—This expression for a fuddy-duddy actually originated back in Elizabethan times, when pirates were hung and buried on the muddy tidal flats of the Thames River so that, "Their foul bodies could not be found or their souls accounted for at resurrection time." (Also see Pirate.)

Stinkpotter—This is the (more affectionate) term that sail-boaters use for a power-boater, when the latter charges by leaving a huge wake and noxious fumes. (Also see Blow-boater and Windjammer.)

Stowaway—This nautical term is used for an illegal passenger who hides onboard to escape or to gain free passage aboard a vessel.

Stowing—This is the proper nautical term for storing items in an orderly, proper, and safe manner aboard a vessel.

Strake—This is a nautical term for a line of planks that run from the bow to the stern along the bottom and sides of a wooden-hulled vessel. (Also see Bow, Planking, and Stern.)

Stranded—This nautical term came from when unscrupulous Masters would leave crewmen upon a strand, e.g. a narrow strip of land, just to avoid paying them after a long voyage. It is sometimes also used to refer to somebody who was shipwrecked. (Also see Castaway and Master.)

Striking The Flag—International law requires that warships fly their ensign (flag) before firing upon an enemy, and it is recognized that a warship surrenders if she lowers (strikes) her flag. It is also an offense to continue to fire on a vessel that has done so, unless she indicates by her other  actions (such as firing or trying to escape) that she has not actually surrendered. Nailing your flag to the mast is a traditional sign of defiance, and indicates that one's colors will not be struck and one's vessel will never surrender. *Trivial Tidbit*—Contrary to popular belief, showing a white flag does not in itself indicate surrender, but is simply a request for a cease-fire so negotiations may take place. One's opponent might not always grant such a request, so don't get too confident! (Also see Ensign and Mast.) (Photograph of Artwork by T.O. Davidson Courtesy of the Naval Historical Center)

Stringer—This nautical term refers to a horizontal structural component that supports the bottom of a vessel.

Stuffing Box—This is the nautical term for a fitting around a propeller shaft designed to keep the water out of the vessel, and also keep the bearings lubricated. (Also see Packing Gland.)

Suck The Monkey—This rather colorful nautical phrase actually referred to surreptitiously drinking spirits out of a coconut (one end of which looks like a monkey's face) by making a hole and using a hollow quill or straw. So now all of you monkeys can relax and come out of the jungle again.

Sundowner—This is (another) nickname for a bullying officer. How many of these guys were there? (Also see Bucko.)

Sun Over the Yardarm—This phrase is a traditional saying among mariners that means it is time for their first drink of the day. It is sometimes also called "elevenses," because when the sun rose above a vessel's yardarm in the northern latitudes it was approximately 11:00 a.m. and was time for the forenoon "stand easy" break on many vessels of the time. (Also see Mariner and Yardarm.)

Swab—This slang term for a sailor originally referred to a mop made out of old rope attached to a wooden handle and used for cleaning a vessel's deck. (Also see, Deck and Rope.)

Swallowing the Anchor—This phrase refers to a mariner leaving the sea and retiring on land. (Also see Mariner.)

Swashbuckler—While movies put a romantic spin on it, in the 16th Century this term actually referred to a swaggering bully, ruffian, or braggart. The word came from combining the term "swash," which meant to make noise by striking something, and the term "buckler," that was a small shield. Back In those days, a Swashbuckler was a mediocre fighter who compensated by banging his sword upon his shield as he strutted through the streets bullying those he met.

T

Tack—Landlubbers might think of a small nail with a big head, but this nautical term is used to refer to: (1) the direction in which a vessel sails with respect to the wind, e.g., a starboard tack, (2) changing the direction in which a vessel is headed by turning her bow through the wind, and (3) the lower forward corner of a triangular sail. *Trivial Tidbit*—For you power boaters, sailing vessels do not sail directly into the wind, but tack on a zigzag course…just to annoy you. (Also see Bow, Forward. And Starboard [Side].)

Tackle—(pronounced tay-kel) This is the nautical term for gear or equipment that may be used on board a vessel to increase mechanical advantage, exert more power, etc.

Taffrail—The nautical term refers to an after rail at a vessel's stern. (Also see Pushpit and Stern.)

Taffrail Log—This is the nautical term for a device that uses a propeller towed through the water astern of a vessel to measure her speed and the distance she has traveled. (Also see Astern and Knot.)

Taken Aback—Today we use this phrase to describe a person at a momentary loss after being jolted by an unexpected event or unpleasant news, but it also refers to when a sudden wind shift (or an inattentive helmsman) causes a vessel's sails to be blown back against her masts. When "taken aback" in such a way, a vessel could be in serious danger of having her masts break and becoming virtually helpless. This is not good! (Also see Mast.)

Taken Down A Peg—This phrase originated from the custom of Admirals and other officers flying their own flags on vessels in which they were embarked. Senior officers' flags were flown higher up on the mast than subordinates, and all such flags were positioned using pegs. If the onboard "pecking order" changed, one's flag might be taken down a peg or two. We currently use this phrase to mean deflating the ego of somebody (who probably deserves it). (Also see Admiral.)

Taking A Walk Up Ladder Lane And Down Hawser Street—This is a rather descriptive nautical term for being hanged. Think about it! (Also see Hawser and Ladder.)

Taking The Wind Out Of One's Sails—We currently use this term to mean getting the best of another person in an argument, but it originally referred to the maneuver in which one sailing vessel passes close enough on the windward side of another to block their wind, causing them to lose headway and maneuverability. A dastardly trick, you scallywag! (Also see Becalm and Windward.)

Tall Ship—Technically, this phrase is used for a sailing vessel whose masts are in segments, e.g., lower, top, or topgallant, for strength and to make them more manageable for partial removal and/or repairs. (Also see Mast.)

Tarpaulin—Long before there were plastic "tarps," this was the nautical term for: (1) a piece of canvas impregnated with tar that was used to cover hatches, etc., and (2) early sailors hats that were made out of similarly tarred or painted cloth. (Also see Hatches and Jack Tar.)

Tattoo—This comes from the Tahitian word *tatau* that means, "to mark," but some sailor's tattoos have more significance that just body art. An anchor tattoo might identify an Atlantic sailor, while one who has sailed around Cape Horn could sport one of a full-rigged ship. Dragons were popular among those who had been in the Far East, while a tattoo of a turtle might mean the wearer had crossed the line. A tattoo of a pig on one foot and a rooster on the other were believed to protect sailors from drowning by helping get them to shore quickly, because neither animal likes the water that much. And last but not least, the word "Hold" tattooed upon the knuckles of one hand and the word "Fast" upon the knuckles of the other hand were believed to help sailors better hang onto the vessel's rigging. (Also see Crossing The Line.)

Telltales—This is a nautical term for yarns, ribbons, or other lightweight materials often attached to a vessel's rigging or sails to indicate the wind's action and/or direction.

Tender—This nautical term is used for: (1) a small boat often used to carry equipment, supplies, or personnel between shore and a larger vessel, (2) describing any vessel that lacks stability, and (3) an individual who stands by in a precautionary or a watchful capacity, e.g. a line tender. (Also see Boat, Lighter, and Line.)

The Devil To Pay—These days, we still use this phrase to mean an unpleasant experience. This original phrase was, "The devil to pay and no pitch hot." Most believe that the devil in this case referred to one of the more difficult seams in a wooden ship's hull to pay (caulk) using hot pine pitch, called "tar." It was an unpleasant and difficult job that was  despised by sailors. (Also see Between The Devil And The Deep.) (Figure Courtesy of the US Navy)

The Tie That Binds—We currently use this phrase when referring to a strong common bond or a lasting relationship, but many believe it was originally used for the short chain that attaches a vessel's fore and main yards to their respective masts. (Also see Mast and Yard.)

The Whole Nine Yards—Between the 1500s and the early 1800s, a "typical" square-rigged ship had three masts with three primary yards on each mast. When all of her square sails were flying, she had "the whole nine yards" involved. Others insist that this phrase comes from the fact that such vessels were not fully committed to a tack until their "ninth yard" was changed over, allowing some Captains to fool less experienced ones in battle into thinking they were turning. (Also see Captain, Mast, Tack, and Yard.)

Three Mile Limit—This was once the distance from shore over which a nation had legal jurisdiction, and was considered the boundary of the "high seas." At the time this was international law, three miles was about the longest range of any nation's most powerful shore guns. But in 1988, the Territorial Sea Proclamation established the high seas boundary at twelve miles offshore.

Three Sheets To The Wind—In sailing terms, sheets are lines used to control the sails. If the main, windward, and leeward sheets are let go, the sails are said to be "in the wind," and a vessel in such a condition may stagger like a drunken soldier...but never a sailor. (Also see Lines and Sheets.)

Tidy—This commonly used word comes from a nautical term that refers to a person being as methodical as the tides.

Toasting—Toasting might not have had a nautical origin, but it was enthusiastically practiced both ashore and at sea. Some say this term evolved from the medieval practice of putting a piece of spiced toast into the goblet of wine that was passed among one's guests prior to being offered to a high ranking lady or an honored person. Others maintain the term came from an English tradition of dipping burned bread into a tankard of ale to improve the taste of the latter. Captain Bucko prefers

the premise that since many waterfront taverns were not the cleanest of all spots, it was often prudent to lay a piece of bread or toast over the top of one's mug simply to minimize the unexpected addition of foreign particles or proteins, e.g., bugs or worse. (Photograph of Sketch by T. Dart Walker Courtesy of the Naval Historical Center)

Toe The Line!—This was the command given at least once a week (and often on Sundays) when the crews of British warships were ordered to fall in for inspection with their toes upon particular lines made by their vessel's deck planks. On other occasions, ship's boys or midshipmen might have to "toe the line" as a punishment for minor infractions such as fidgeting or talking at an inappropriate time, and could be required to remain for hours in all weather conditions. (Also see Planking.)

To Go On Account—This actually originated as the old nautical phrase "to go on the account," which meant to become a pirate. Yo-ho, Yo-ho, a pirate's life for me…(Also see Pirate.)

Tom Cox's Traverse—There is a question about who Tom Cox was, but this nautical phrase means somebody who bustles about doing very little. Sometimes it is appended by words like, "running twice around the scuttlebutt and once around the longboat." Most of us have met a Tom Cox. (Also see Scuttlebutt.)

Ton—Some believe that this unit of weight evolved from the *tun*, a large cask that held 252 gallons and was frequently used in reference to a vessel's cargo carrying ability. In early shipping jargon, a 100-ton vessel could stow 100 *tuns* in her hold. (Also see Hold.)

Topside—This nautical term is used to refer to: (1) being on or above a vessel's main deck, and (2) those portions of a vessel's sides that lie between the waterline and her deck. (Also see Deck, Main Deck, and Waterline.)

Touch And Go—These days we use this phrase to indicate being in a tenuous position, but it originally referred to when a vessel actually touched the bottom but got back off again. Whew!

Transom—This term refers to vertical athwartship planking, plastic, or steel plates that form the stern and close off a vessel's sides. If you have an outboard engine, consider putting it here! (Also see Athwartships, Outboard, Planking, and Stern.)

Trim—This nautical term means to adjust a vessel's sails, loading, rudder, and/or other control systems, e.g., trim tabs, to relieve stresses and/or to operate more advantageously.

True Colors—This comes from the practice of warships flying their own national flags (ensigns) when engaged in naval battles. (Also see Bamboozle, Ensign, and Showing One's True Colors.)

Trying Times—We often use this phrase to describe a difficult period, but it originated from when vessels used a triangularly shaped "trysail" during particularly tumultuous weather conditions.

Turning A Blind Eye—This expression for purposely ignoring something actually came from when Admiral Nelson won the Battle of Copenhagen in 1801, after he deliberately held his telescope to his blind eye so that he could not see a signal that he preferred to disregard. Signal, what signal?

Twenty-One Gun Salute—Now days we may render twenty-one guns salutes to a national flag, current and former Presidents and Presidents-elect, sovereigns, chiefs of state, and members of reigning royal families. We also fire twenty-one gun salutes on certain national holidays, including Washington's Birthday, the Fourth of July, Presidents' Day, and at noon on Memorial Day. *Trivial Tidbit*—With the prior approval of the Secretary, US Navy vessels may render gun salutes for naval officers as follows: Admiral (17 guns), Vice Admiral (15 guns), Rear Admiral, upper half (13 guns), and Rear Admiral, lower half (11 guns). (Also see Gun Salutes.)

U

Under Foot—We use this phrase to mean that something is in the way, but it originally was the nautical term for when an anchor is under the vessel's forefoot, and its rode is nearly vertical. (Also see Forefoot and Rode.)

Under The Weather—A crewmember standing watch on the "weather side" of the vessel is subject to the wind and spray, and is said to be "under the weather." We currently use this phrase to mean an unpleasant condition.

Underway—A vessel is said to be underway when her anchor has been weighed or her lines cast off. This should not be confused with making way. (Also see Cast Off, Making Way, and Weigh.)

Unfurl—This nautical term means to unfold or to unroll a sail. Surprisingly enough, it is the opposite of the term "furl". (Also see Furl.)

Union Jack—This is the nautical term for a replica of the blue field (union) of stars from the United States flag recently flown by US Navy vessels between 0800 and sunset while at anchor, until the Secretary of the Navy ordered them to once again fly the First Navy Jack during the war on terrorism beginning on Patriot's Day, 11 September 2002. (Also see First Navy Jack.) (Figure Courtesy of the US Navy)

Union Jack

Unreeved His Lifeline—This is another nautical expression that mariners use for a shipmate who has died and gone on to Davy Jones' Locker (if lost or buried at sea) or Fiddler's Green (if buried ashore). It's better than "He kicked the bucket." (Also see Cut His Painter, Davy Jones' Locker, Fiddler's Green, Gone Aloft, Mariner, and Shipmate.)

V

Victuals—(often pronounced vittels). This term for edibles actually has nautical origins dating back to 1665, with the formation of the *Victualing Department of the Royal Navy*. Before then, individual Captains and Pursers of Royal Navy ships made their own arrangements for their vessel's provisions, and sometimes skimmed off a little money for themselves in the process. (Also see Captain and Purser.)

W

Waist—This is the nautical term for that part of a sailing vessel's upper deck between her fore and main masts, or between the forecastle and quarterdeck on other vessels. (Also see Forecastle, Foremast, Main Mast, and Quarterdeck.)

Waister—This nautical term refers to an incompetent person or one worn out after many years at sea. They were often given menial jobs to do in the area of the vessel's waist. (Also see Waist.)

Wake—This nautical term refers to the waves, eddies, and other disturbances created by a vessel's passage through the water. If you are moving ahead, this comes out of the stern. (Also see Stern.)

Wardroom—This was originally called the *Wardrobe Room*. In the early days it was a secure space where officers kept their spare uniforms, and was also used to stow any loot from captured enemy vessels. Over the years, the term evolved into Wardroom and became the space in a vessel in which her officers gather and eat. (Also see Officer and Officer's Mess.)

Warming the Bell—This nautical phrase refers to the practice of striking eight bells slightly before the end of one's watch. It is currently used to refer to doing something a bit prematurely. (Also see Ships' Bells.)

Washed Out—We often use this phrase to indicate failure, but some say it came from when messages passed by signal flags were recorded upon slate tablets that were cleaned with wet sponges after such messages had been passed to the proper recipients or cancelled.

Watches—A traditional shipboard watch schedule may consist of: a midwatch from 0000-0400, a morning watch from 0400-0800, a forenoon watch from 0800-1200, an afternoon watch from 1200-1600, a first dog watch from 1600-1800, a second dog watch from 1800-2000, and an evening watch from 2000-2400. On board some merchant vessels there may be only two watches, sometimes called larboard and starboard. (Also see Dog Watch, Larboard, and Starboard [Side].)

Waterline—This nautical term refers to the water level on a vessel's hull when she has a full complement of personnel, cargo, and stores on board. (Also see Load Line.)

Way—This is the nautical term used to describe movement of a vessel through the water, e.g., headway (ahead), sternway (astern), or leeway (sideways). (Also see Ahead, Astern, and Making Way.)

Weather Deck(s)—This nautical term refers to any deck without overhead protection from the weather. Try to stay off these during heavy weather, unless you like long-distance swimming. (Also see Deck.)

Weigh—This nautical term means to raise the anchor off of the bottom. (Also see Aweigh.)

Wharf—This is the nautical term for a man-made structure that is parallel to the shoreline, and is often used for making vessels fast, loading/offloading cargo, embarking/debarking passengers, etc. (Also see Debark, Embark, Fast, Finger Pier, Pier, and Quay.)

When My Ship Comes In—This was actually a legal phrase as far back as 1536, whereby individuals promised payment of a debt within a specified number of days after the safe arrival of their ships.

Where Away?—This is a query typically addressed to a vessel's lookout inquiring about the bearing and the distance of an object that he or she has sighted and reported. (Also see Bearing,)

Whip—It may surprise you to discover that this is not about flogging! Instead, this term refers to binding the strands of a line or rope with a small cord to prevent fraying. (Also see Line and Rope.)

Whistling For Wind—This expression is based on the old nautical superstition that whistling when becalmed would cause the wind to rise, and that whistling when there was already a breeze might result in a storm. Today the phrase is commonly used to mean, "no chance!" (Also see Becalm.)

Widow Maker—This was the nickname that sailors gave to the bowsprit of sailing vessels, because so many of them lost their lives by falling overboard while working in that area. (Also see Bowsprit.)

Winch—This is a term for a device with a horizontal drum upon which a line, cable, or chain is wound to assist in hoisting, hauling, etc. (Also see Windlass.)

Windfall—We currently use this to indicate an unexpected stroke of good luck. In nautical terms, it may be used to describe a sudden offshore wind that can provide a vessel more leeway. Another explanation says that during the reign of George III, English landowners were not permitted to cut down any trees larger than 24 inches in diameter, which "belonged to the King" and were reserved for building Royal Navy ships. The law did not apply to any trees that were blown down however, which the landowners could sell for a profit. That was a real windfall! (Also see Leeway.)

Windlass—This nautical term refers to a mechanical device with one or more horizontal drums used to pull in or pay out an anchor rode, chain, etc. (Also see Winch.)

Windjammer—This was the general term for large square-rigged vessels common during the waning days of commercial sailing, but crewmen of early steam-powered vessels originally meant it as an insult. After they heard their vessels' nickname, the crews of the windjammers began to call the steamships "stinkpotters," and today blow-boaters still use that term for people who want to get to the other side of a pond in less than a day. (Also see Blowboater and Stinkpotter.)

Windward—This nautical term is used to refer to both: (1) the upwind direction, and (2) the side of a vessel upon which the wind blows, also sometimes called her "weather" side. (Also see Leeward.)

X

Xebec—This refers to an old type of three-mast vessel once used in the Mediterranean. And I'll bet some of you did not think that Captain Bucko could find a nautical term that began with the letter X!

Y

Yacht—(pronounced *yaht*) This nautical term refers a sailboat or powerboat that is used for pleasure, not a working boat or a military vessel. The name comes from the Dutch *jacht*, for speedy vessels with comfortable quarters that carried very important persons from place to place. Some insist that a yacht should be at least sixty-five feet in length, but most of them already own vessels that are longer than sixty-five feet. *Trivial Tidbit*—A "mega-yacht" is sometimes defined as a yacht that is owned by a person with way too much money. (Also see Boat and Sailboat.)

Yankee—This actual origin of this nickname is not entirely clear, but some say it originated from the reputation early American sea captains had among the Dutch as being very hard to please. The Dutch, who were also known for being frugal themselves, referred to these Americans as *yankers,* or wranglers. Over the years, the word evolved into Yankee.

Yard—This is the nautical term for a spar or a long piece of timber that tapers slightly toward its ends and is hung by its center to a vessel's mast to support square-rigged sails. (Also see Mast, Spar, and Yardarm.)

Yardarm—This nautical term is used to describe the outboard end of a vessel's yard. (Also see Outboard, Yard, and Yardarm And Yardarm.)

Yardarm And Yardarm—This nautical phrase refers to when vessels lie so close alongside each other that their yardarms cross or touch. (Also see Close Aboard, Board And Board, and Yardarm.)

Yarn—This is the nautical term for a sea story or a tale, but it is also a component of a rope. (Also see Spinning Yarns and Rope.)

Yawl—This term refers to a two-mast sailboat that has a relatively short mizzenmast located abaft of her helm. *Trivial Tidbit*—If the mizzenmast of a similarly-rigged vessel is located forward of her helm, she is usually referred to as a ketch. (Also see Aft, Forward, Ketch, and Mizzenmast.) (Figure Courtesy of J. Wilkinson)

Yawl

You Scratch My Back And I'll Scratch Yours—This old phrase came from an informal pact among mariners when flogging was more common. It basically meant that if one person took it easy when whipping another, the favor would be returned. (Also see Cat O' Nine Tails and Mariner.)

Z

Zephyr—This is the nautical term used for a very gentle breeze. (Also see Cat's Paw.)

Zincs—This is the term used for "sacrificial" pieces of (guess what kind of) metal that are commonly used to help reduce saltwater corrosion. Let's hear it for the unselfish zincs!

SO IN SUMMARY...

"*Pipe down, matey! Just **toe the line** and mind the **scuttlebutt**. You are not so **groggy, under the weather,** or **three sheets to the wind** that a **cup of Joe** and a **square meal** won't make you feel **first rate**. But if the **Skipper** catches you **chewing the fat** it will be **touch and go,** and if he does not like the **cut of your jib** you might find yourself **over a barrel**. If you keep **above board,** you will **by and large** not be **at loggerheads** or have **the devil to pay**. So if you **know the ropes,** you **son of a gun,** everything will be **hunky dory**. You will not be **taken aback,** and can **start with a clean slate**. Now do not **let the cat out of the bag,** just because we have come to the **bitter end** of this **yarn**. And if you do not want to **splice the main brace** with Captain Bucko, you can just **get knotted!**"*

CONGRATULATIONS, SHIPMATE!

You have successfully navigated the treacherous rocks and shoals of *Captain Bucko's Nauti-Words Handbook* and are undoubtedly a much better person for it. You have ventured into the realm of Davy Jones, and you have proven once again that...

"Etymology can be fun!"

I hope you have enjoyed reading about the fascinating nautical origins of literally hundreds of everyday expressions, and have learned a little about some of those nautical terms that may have puzzled you. It has been a pleasure having you on board, and I look forward to our next voyage.

—*Captain Bucko*

ADDITIONAL RESOURCES

Other sources that readers may find useful for additional information about the nautical terms and phrases discussed in this publication include:

Common Knots Web Site (http://neropes.com/pleasure_marine/knots.html)

Dictionary of Sea Terms Web Site (1841/1851) (http://www.people.fas.harvard.edu/~morris3/DanaSFLex.html

Early American Sailing Ships Web Site (http://www.keyshistory.org/ASS-Amer-Sail-Ships.html)

Glossary of Nautical Terms (circa. 1814) Web Site (http://www.psych.usyd.edu.au/vbb/woronora/maritime/Glossary.html

Guide To The Tall Ships Web Site (http://www.sitesalive.com/cal/tg/private/caltgTallShip.pdf)

MARISAFE Boating Dictionary Web Site (http://www.marisafe.com/resources/boatdictionary.asp?mode=browse&term=A&did=1025)

Nautical Know How, Glossary of Nautical Terms Web Site (http://www.boatsafe.com/nauticalknowhow/gloss.htm)

NOAA Photo Library (http://www.photolib.noaa.gov/)

Shipbuilding Terms Web Site
(http://collections.ic.gc.ca/vessels/terms.htm)

Terms, Traditions and Customs of the Naval Service Web Site
(http://www.bluejacket.com/tradition.htm)

US Coast Guard Glossary of Boating Terms Web Site
(http://www.uscgboating.org/glossary.htm)

US Navy, Chief of Naval Information Web Site
(http://www.chinfo.navy.mil/navpalib/traditions/html/navyterm.html)

US Naval Historical Center Web Site
(http://www.history.navy.mil/nhc3.htm,
http://www.history.navy.mil/trivia/trivia03.htm)

USS Constitution Web Site (http://www.ussconstitution.navy.mil/)

0-595-31529-1

Printed in the United States
28231LVS00004B/412

9 780595 315291